THE ONTARIO ALTERNATIVE BUDGET PAPERS

What We Need and How We Fund It

Jobs, Education, Health, Local Government, Child Care, Social Services, Public Housing, The Environment

Developed by a coalition of unions and community-action groups brought together by the Ontario Federation of Labour

An Our Schools/Our Selves Title

James Lorimer & Company Ltd., Publishers
Toronto, 1997

Copyright © Our Schools/Our Selves Education Foundation
October, 1997

For subscribers to *Our Schools/Our Selves: a magazine for Canadian education activists*, this is issue #53, the 5th of Volume 8.

The subscription series Our Schools/Our Selves (ISSN 0840-7339) is published six times a year. Publication Mail Registration Number 8010. Mailed at Centre Ville, Montreal, Quebec.

Canadian Cataloguing in Publication Data

Main entry under title:

The Ontario alternative budget papers : what we need and how we fund it

(Our schools/our selves , ISSN 0840–7339 ; no. 24)
Includes bibliographical references.
ISBN   1–55028–594–7

1. Finance, Public – Canada.   2. Budget – Ontario.
I. Ontario Federation of Labour.   II. Series.

HJ2056.5.05058 1997   336.3'09713   C97–931545–X

Design and typesetting: Tobin MacIntosh.

Cover Design: Nancy Reid.

Our Schools/Our Selves production: Keren Brathwaite, David Clandfield, Lorna Erwin, John Huot, Doug Little, Magda Lewis, Bob Luker, George Martell, Brian Pastoor, Claire Polster, Satu Repo (Executive Editor), Bairu Sium, Harry Smaller.

James Lorimer & Company Ltd., Publishers
35 Britain Street
Toronto M5A 1R7

Printed and bound in Canada by La maîtresse d'école inc., Montreal, Quebec.

Acknowledgements

The 14 budget papers are the result of much reflection and discussion by the Ontario Alternative Budget Working Group and its committees. Special thanks for coordinating and writing individual papers goes to:

Jim Stanford
– Ontario's Job Crisis and its Link to the Provincial Deficit
– Working Down Our Debts: Creating 600,00 Jobs to Rebuild Our Communities
– Ontario 1997–98 Budget Highlights
– The Alternative Federal Budget and its Implications for Ontario

Hugh Mackenzie
– Options for Restoring Ontario's Fiscal Capacity
– Local Government and Public Services in Ontario: Disentanglement or Discombobulation?

John McEwen – Education: Towards Tomorrow

Andy Ranachan – Social Policy: What Are We Willing To Do?

Bill Morris – Housing: Filling the Void

Julie Mathien – Child Care: The Case for Reform

Vicky Smallman, Maureen Wall & Mark Rosenfeld – Post Secondary Education: An Alternative Vision

THE ONTARIO ALTERNATIVE BUDGET PAPERS

Mark Winfield and the Ontario Environmental Protection Group	– The Environment: Our Future, Our Health
Dan Benedict	– Health Care: The Crisis Continues
Ross McClellan	– Ontario's Diminished Fiscal Capacity

The Ontario Federation of Labour has provided a secretariat to the OAB, production and printing services, and the staff services of Ross McClellan, co-ordinator and Jill Michalko, administrative support.

The Ontario Alternative Budget Working Group

Susan Eagle, *Co-Chair*	Ontario Social Safety NetWork
Hugh Mackenzie, *Co-Chair*	United Steelworkers of America
Ross McClellan, *Co-ordinator*	Ontario Federation of Labour
Greg Albo	Professor, York University
Dan Benedict	Ontario Health Coalition
Geoff Bickerton	Canadian Union of Postal Workers
Sheila Block	United Steelworkers of America
Andrea Calver	Ontario Coalition for Social Justice
Wayne Cushman	Ontario Secondary School Teachers Federation
Jonathan Eaton	Union of Needletrades, Industrial and Textile Employees
Larry French	Ontario Secondary School Teachers Federation
Jay Kaufman	Consultant
Tim Little	Ontario Public Service Employees Union
John MacLennan	Unemployed Workers Council
George Martell	Ontario Education Alliance

ACKNOWLEDGEMENTS

Michael Mendelson	Senior Scholar, Caledon Institute of Social Policy
Bill Morris	The Co-operative Housing Federation
Josefina Moruz	United Food and Commercial Workers Union
Keith Newman	Communications Energy and Paperworkers Union
Jim Onyschuk	Ontario Public Service Employees Union
Andy Ranachan	Metro Network for Social Justice
Marilyn Roycroft	Federation of Women's Teachers Association of Ontario
Matt Sanger	Canadian Union of Public Employees
Chris Schenk	Ontario Federation of Labour
Michelle Sherwood	Service Employees International Union
Myer Siemiatycki	Social Planning Council of Metro Toronto
Vicky Smallman	Canadian Federation of Students
Jim Stanford	Canadian Autoworkers Union

Contents

THE ONTARIO ALTERNATIVE BUDGET PAPERS

Acknowledgements	iii
Preface	9
Introduction	12

Part I – Austerity and Government Finances

Chapter 1   23
       Ontario's Diminished Fiscal Capacity

Chapter 2   31
       Options for Restoring Ontario's Fiscal Capacity

Part II – Fighting the Jobs Deficit

Chapter 3   50
       Ontario's Jobs Crisis and its Link to the Provincial Daficit

Chapter 4   73
       Working Down our Debts:
       Creating 600,000 Jobs to Rebuild our Communities

Part III – Fighting the Jobs Deficit

Chapter 5   93
       Education: Towards Tomorrow

Chapter 6	114
Post Secondary Education: An Alternative Vision	
Chapter 7	128
Child Care: The Case for Reform	
Chapter 8	134
The Environment: Our Future, Our Health	
Chapter 9	149
Health Care: The Crisis Continues	
Chapter 10	158
Social Policy: What are We Willing to Do?	
Chapter 11	168
Housing: Filling the Void	
Chapter 12	187
Local Government and Public Services in Ontario: Disentanglement or Discombobulation?	
Chapter 13	206
Ontario 1997–98 Budget Highlights	
Chapter 14	212
The Alternative Federal Budget and its Implications for Ontario	

Preface

The Ontario Alternative Budget Working Group is a coalition of labour, social action, community and church groups which have come together to develop alternatives to the Common Sense Revolution of the Conservative government of Mike Harris. We are part of the growing legion of Ontarians who are determined to fight the Harris agenda.

The Working Group established six framework objectives:

1. We will produce an Alternative Ontario Budget which is credible, concrete and realistic while at the same time visionary, inspiring hope in the real possibility of progressive reform.

2. The project will focus on the underlying causes of Ontario's fiscal and economic problems, and attempt to address them as directly as possible.

3. Ontario's large operating deficit is unsustainable. A strategy to achieve full funding of government programs with, over time, a balanced operating budget is essential, both in principle and to win broad public credibility.

4. Jobs and the economy will be a major focus of the budget, with an emphasis on youth unemployment, and an initiative to set economic standards or goals for Ontario.

5. A second focus will be to promote a vision of the value of the public sector, the importance of the social safety net and the need to preserve essential public services. The non-profit, cooperative or third sector of the economy will be encouraged to play an increasing role.
6. All provincial budgets exist in the context of Federal monetary and fiscal policy. We will assume the essential need for parallel progressive reform at the Federal level, and demonstrate the beneficial impact of the Alternative Federal Budget upon this province.

On April 24, 1997, the Working Group launched the Alternative Budget process. Over the next six to eight months, we will sponsor meetings, workshops and discussions across the province about the issues raised in this document. Out of this process of open dialogue will come a concrete Ontario Alternative Budget for 1998–99.

The purpose of the papers in this volume is to stimulate discussion. Many of the papers set out ambitious goals for expanded services with price tags. A number of alternative budget plans are developed to show how these goals could be funded.

It is well more than a decade since Canada joined other countries locked in the grip of neo-liberal economic ideology. At the bidding of Canada's business elite, two successive federal governments and now, with a vengeance, the Harris government in Ontario have introduced wave after wave of programs and policies designed to downgrade the public sector of the economy and to liberate the free market.

The liberation of free market forces has meant deregulation, privatization and massive public sector downsizing. Not since the Great Depression of the 1930s have Canadians been so exposed to the harsh effects of unrestrained free market forces, which are now wreaking exactly the same kind of havoc in Ontario as they have elsewhere in the past. The supporters of the Ontario Alternative Budget reject the dog-eat-dog society that corporate Canada seems determined to inflict on the province.

We call for a return to the practical idealism of economic policies that emphasize full employment and social security. At the same time, we recognize the need to meet the challenge of the new economy and the mass unemployment it has unleashed. We look for solutions based on a renewed sense of community and social solidarity. And we expect creative leadership from our democratically elected governments that will find solutions in partnership with local communities to the very real problems that market forces have inflicted on us.

With the papers in this volume, the Ontario Alternative Budget Working Group intends to launch an Alternative Budget process that involves as many people as possible in the search for a common program. These papers are viewed as the framework for a discussion about the choices Ontario can, and must, make if we are to recover from our current misfortunes. All budgets – including the ones that plague us now – are about choices that involve our fundamental values and priorities. We invite all those who seek to create a better world to join with us in beginning a process that will help build a more democratic and equalitarian society.

Introduction

The Ontario Alternative Budget Working Group is an alliance of organizations concerned about the future of public services in Ontario. Formed during the winter of 1997, it includes representatives of organized labour, interfaith groups, students, teachers, childcare advocates, the cooperative housing sector, social justice coalitions, health care workers and environmentalists. It also includes, as active participants, a number of the individuals who have been involved in the preparation of the Alternative Federal Budget for the past three years.

The members of the Working Group share a vision of a system of public services in Ontario that contributes actively to the improvement of the quality of life for everyone in Ontario. We believe in a strong public sector able to meet current needs and respond to changes in the economic and social environment. We do not share the view that the public sector is a drag on the well-being of Ontarians. On the contrary, we believe that a dynamic and effective public sector is the critical factor that has given Ontario and its major cities a quality of life that is admired around the world. Threats to public services in Ontario, like those posed by the Harris government, are threats to the foundation of the society we want for ourselves and want to pass on to our children.

Each of us is forced to deal with particular aspects of the Harris revolution in our own sphere of activity. What brings us together is a recognition that there can be no effective response to any individual element of the Harris program without addressing the overall fiscal and budgetary issues that are the public rationale for that program. The first step is a broadly based discussion of the alternative courses of action that might be open to the province. We see the release of the 1997 Ontario Alternative Budget papers as the beginning of a process that will lead to a comprehensive alternative budget for the next fiscal year. In the years that follow an objective is to present an alternative vision for the future of public finance and public services in Ontario.

For the past two years, Ontarians have been fed a steady diet of "there is no alternative" to the most draconian destruction of public services ever undertaken in Canada. We have been told that Ontario's finances are in crisis. We have been told that the crisis was caused by runaway spending on social services. We have been told that the only way to resolve this "crisis" is to impose dramatic cutbacks in every area of public service in Ontario.

The list of "no alternative" transformations includes: virtual elimination of Ontario's system of environmental monitoring and enforcement; widespread closures of hospitals imposed without public debate or input; a "reform" of provincial/local government relationships that has destroyed partnerships built up over decades and that will shift as much as a billion dollars on to the local property tax; declarations that Ontario spends "too much" on education, indicating future cuts that will further undermine an already battered educational system; the elimination of funding for countless community-based organizations that are the foundation for Ontario's network of voluntary and non-profit activities; massive cuts in the living standards of the most vulnerable people in our society; and regulatory changes that benefit the powerful and penalize the vulnerable.

In an atmosphere of crisis, the argument of "no alternatives" can be compelling. As compelling as it may be, however, it is a deceitful argument that is intended to mislead. It is not true that there is no alternative to the policies of the Harris government. There are choices open to Ontario, even in the late 1990s.

The Alternative Ontario Budget Papers are intended to contribute to an informed debate about real alternatives – to provoke discussion and raise important questions of public policy. Even at this early stage of our alternative budget process, we have been able to expose important contradictions, distortions and outright falsehoods that lie at the heart of the rationale for the Harris program.

The cornerstone of the Alternative Budget are the papers dealing with Ontario's fiscal situation and economic performance. Dealing aggressively and effectively with Ontario's budgetary situation is fundamental to any alternative vision. Current levels of debt and deficit are simply not sustainable. A sensible response to that imperative, however, must be based on an understanding of the factors that led to the situation we now find ourselves in.

The papers in Part I deal with Ontario's fiscal capacity problem. The Harris government repeats ad nauseam that Ontario's deficit and debt problems were created by out-of-control public spending. The evidence does not support that claim.

The first paper, "Ontario's Diminished Fiscal Capacity," demonstrates that program spending relative to the size of the Ontario economy in the 1990s was in the range that would be expected in the deepest recession since the 1930s. The chief culprit turns out to have been policies of successive federal governments. Provincial fiscal capacity was not only undermined by federal abandonment of traditional commitments to social programs, it was also hurt by unrealistically low inflation targets, creating high unemployment and high interest rates.

The second paper, "Options for Restoring Ontario's Fiscal Capacity," presents four fiscal scenarios as alternatives to the Harris agenda. Each scenario is designed to achieve a balanced budget no more than one year later than Harris has projected. And each takes as its starting point the elimination of the unfair and wasteful Harris tax cut. The first scenario demonstrates conclusively that there is no fiscal crisis in Ontario. This flatline spending scenario shows that, without

INTRODUCTION

the tax cut and using consensus forecasts of economic growth, no spending cuts would have been required to balance the budget on the schedule proposed by Harris in the so-called Common Sense Revolution. All of the budget-cutting pain and all of the deterioration in public services now being inflicted on Ontario can be laid at the feet of the tax-cut promise. Even in the flatline spending scenario, however, the quality of public services in Canada would continue to be undermined by inflation and population growth.

In the second scenario, we are able to maintain our level of commitment to public services in Ontario with a tax package amounting to $1.7 billion. This amount could be raised, for example, by broadening the sales tax base to include business services, restoring historic levels of tax on tobacco products and eliminating costly and ineffective tax breaks in the Employer Health Tax. This scenario maintains real per capita program spending at its 1995–96 level.

In the third scenario, we restore the public economy to the share of the total economy it held during the last period of relatively full employment in 1989–90. The fact that this scenario requires tax increases amounting to $3.2 billion illustrates clearly the profoundly negative impact of federal policies on Ontario's fiscal capacity. This scenario simply restores provincial public services to a level slightly below their long-term average share of the economy and requires over $3 billion in tax increases to hit fiscal targets.

The fourth scenario is included to illustrate the positive impact that would result from federal policies committed to full employment and a cooperative approach to funding national programs. It shows what Ontario's fiscal picture would look like if policies like those advanced in the Alternative Federal Budget were in place. In this scenario, Ontario could maintain real per capita spending with no tax increase.

While these four scenarios meet the overriding constraint of bringing the budget into balance, they have very different implications for public services in Ontario, and therefore very different implications for our quality of life. Which of the competing scenarios emerges from our debate will determine the extent to which we can afford to fund the ideas that emerge on the public policy side of the equation in Parts II and III.

The papers in Part II focus on the theme of fighting the jobs deficit. "Ontario's Job Crisis and its link to the Provincial Deficit" presents a detailed and comprehensive analysis of the state of the Ontario economy, and underlines the links between the performance of the economy and the budget. It demonstrates that the employment rate – a measure of the proportion of the working-age population that is employed – has not increased since the last recession. It also shows that much of the employment growth since then has been part-time. In particular, there is no evidence that the Harris government's much ballyhooed tax cut has had any positive impact on the Ontario economy whatsoever.

The fourth paper, "Working Down Our Debts," complements the third. It discusses new ideas for community-based job creation and economic development in Ontario, and presents a vision of a democratically controlled, community-based initiative to meet community needs and to create badly needed jobs.

The papers in Part III raise issues related to the rebuilding of public services in Ontario in light of the structural changes that have taken place in our economy and society. The first three focus on various aspects of the education and child care systems, from early childhood to post-secondary. We do not share the government's view that the sole purpose of the education system is to prepare children for work. We believe that quality public education is essential for the maintenance of a healthy, civil society. But even within its own narrow terms, the Harris government's education policies collapse from internal contradictions.

Everyone seems to agree that quality investments in education are the most important ones we can make for the economic and social future of our province and country. Despite overwhelming evidence that the early childhood years are the most important for building a skilled and educated workforce for the future, the government has cancelled funding for junior kindergarten and imposed dramatic cuts on the child care system.

The government uses its claim that Ontario spends excessively on education to justify its attack on the organization and funding of the education system. The problem is that this claim is not true. A study of education spending audited by the econometric consulting firm Informetrica shows that Ontario ranks forty-sixth in per pupil spending among state and provincial jurisdictions in North America. New Jersey, often cited by the Harris government as a model of right-wing rectitude, spends 82% more per pupil than Ontario. Ontario is tied for forty-fifth spot for average class size, behind Alabama, Georgia and Mississippi. Even without the Harris cuts, Ontario lags far behind the rest of North America in its investment in our children's future.

The paper on post-secondary education is based on an analysis of the situation in Ontario's system by all of the major stakeholders – students, faculty and administrators. Among their findings: Ontario ranks dead last among Canadian provinces in its spending per student on post-secondary education. For a province that hopes to excel in the age of information technology and knowledge-based workers, this is a pathetic record.

The next paper, "The Environment: Our Future, Our Health," presents an exhaustive review of the impact of the Harris cuts on environmental quality and monitoring in Ontario. We may not have a fiscal crisis, but we certainly have a crisis in environmental management. The Harris government is systematically dismantling the institutions and regulations that have been developed to protect the environment for future generations.

"Heath Care: The Crisis Continues" addresses the chaos being created by the government as it moves across the province dictating the closure of hospitals and other health facilities with no community input or involvement. The government is destroying health care institutions in the name of community-based care, but with no intention of funding the community alternatives. Our public health care system is not only our proudest social policy achievement, it is also a major competitive advantage for Canadian industry. The Harris government is pushing it to the brink of collapse at the same time as it turns over an increasing share of the system to the profit-making health care industry.

"Social Policy: What Are We Willing To Do?" highlights the government's hypocritical retreat from the support of poor children and their families, while claiming that its program will give a break to low and moderate-income Ontarians. Workfare turns out to be nothing more than hot air. The paper documents the growth of poverty in Ontario and sets out a framework for a discussion to forge a new social policy for the province.

"Housing: Filling the Void" focuses on the real crisis that is developing in affordable housing. The only affordable housing that has been built in Ontario in the past fifteen years has been in the non-profit and cooperative sector. That sector has been decimated by funding cuts. Rent controls have effectively been eliminated, making low-income tenants even more vulnerable than they were. And there is absolutely no evidence that the private market, once released from rent controls, will build any housing that is affordable for low- and moderate-income individuals and families. All we can expect from Harris' housing policies is an increase in rents and an increase in homelessness.

"Local Government and Public Services" in Ontario provides an overview of the upheaval created by the province in local government. It points out that the changes underway run in the opposite direction from those recommended by every study that has been done of the provincial/local government relationship in the past fifteen years. The paper also reveals that the government originally overstated by about $700 million the benefit to local governments of provincial funding for education replacing residential property taxes.

Even after it's partial retreat, the overstatement is still $150 million and the total download over $800 million – equivalent to an increase in residential property taxes of approximately 13%. The paper argues that the government has significantly understated the impact of such changes as market value reassessment and education finance reform on individual municipalities and individual taxpayers. Regional averages (claiming relatively modest shifts in taxes and funding) mask significant local impacts from all of these changes. Unless local governments decide to increase residential taxes, the elimination of the business occupancy tax will increase taxes on small businesses by more than 10% while reducing taxes on banks by a little less than 10%.

These papers have been prepared in the hope that they will inform a broader public debate on options for the future in Ontario. We have already learned a great deal. We know that there is no fiscal crisis in Ontario, that the sole reason for the cuts we are now suffering is the need to generate the funds to pay for the Harris tax cut. We know that, despite the government's self-congratulatory rhetoric, Ontario has not recovered from the recession of the early 1990s. We know that Ontario lags far behind other jurisdictions in its commitment to early childhood and post-secondary education and that we rank near the bottom of the heap among states and provinces in North America in elementary and secondary schooling. We know that the Harris government is taking incalculable risks with our environmental future. We know that even the revised version of the Harris Who Does What scheme will result in a net shift of $800 million from the province to the property tax.

Over the next few months, the Ontario Alternative Budget Working Group will be holding public meetings, hearings, educational sessions and forums on alternative fiscal strategies in communities across Ontario. Our goal is to build a broad consensus among people concerned about the future direction of this province for an alternative budgetary and public-policy strategy. We invite all to join us in this effort.

Part I

Austerity and Government Finances

Chapter One

ONTARIO'S DIMINISHED FISCAL CAPACITY

Ontario's Debt

Between 1976 and 1990, Ontario's debt was relatively stable as a percentage of Gross Domestic Product (GDP), falling in the range of 15% to 18%. But in the 1990s, in the aftermath of the worst recession in sixty years, Ontario's debt to GDP ratio dramatically increased. Figure 1.1 demonstrates the extent of the problem.

Figure 1.1   Ontario's Debt as Percentage of GDP, 1976–96

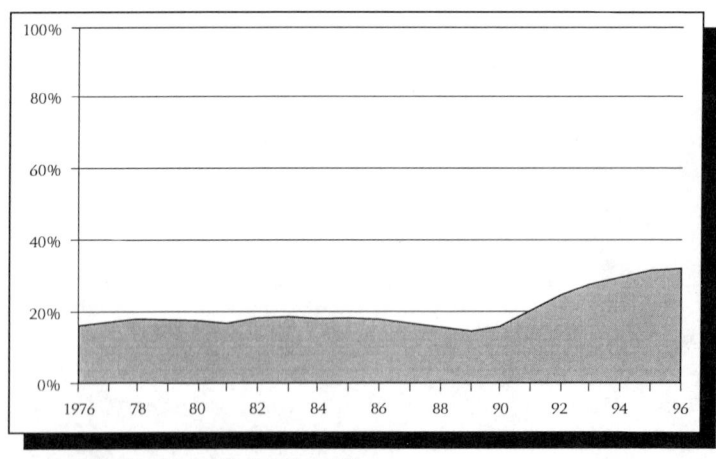

Source: Dominion Bond Rating Service, Nov. 1996

After moving with the business cycle in the range of 15% to 20% from 1976 to 1991, the ratio more than doubled, from 15% in the earliest stages of the recession in mid-1989 to 32% in 1995-96. Debt levels that are this high, relative to the size of the provincial economy, are clearly not sustainable. A growing debt-to-GDP requires that an increasing proportion of the provincial budget be devoted to public debt interest payments. When interest rates exceed the rate of economic growth, as they have for most of the past ten years, the problem becomes even worse.[1] At $8.7 billion, Ontario's public debt interest payment is the province's third largest budget item.

Budgets need to be in balance on average over the business cycle to prevent the public sector from becoming totally mortgaged to banks and international money-lenders. These institutions are the principal beneficiaries of Ontario's huge annual interest payments. The increasing share of the provincial budget that goes to interest payments causes a number of serious problems. It makes it harder to pay for public programs. It forces taxes up even when program spending is not increasing. It reduces the flexibility of the government to fund new social and economic programs in times of recession or dislocation. It transfers wealth from taxpayers to money-lenders.

The question is not whether to respond to these fiscal pressures, but how. In making choices about how to respond, it is important to understand the factors that created fiscal pressures in the first place.

Program Spending

The central justification for the Harris attack on provincial public services is that Ontario's budget deficits were caused by excessive public spending. According to the Harris dogma, out-of-control program spending both created Ontario's fiscal crisis and damaged our economy by crowding out private sector activity. This is simply not true.

As Figure 1.2 demonstrates, program spending as a share of Ontario's economy has been extremely stable over a very long time. In periods of economic recession, program spending has tended to increase slightly relative to GDP, both because the level of need for many public services increases during recessions and because the growth of the economy itself slows dramatically. In periods of recovery, the opposite happens.

Figure 1.2 Program Spending as Percentage of GDP, 1976–97

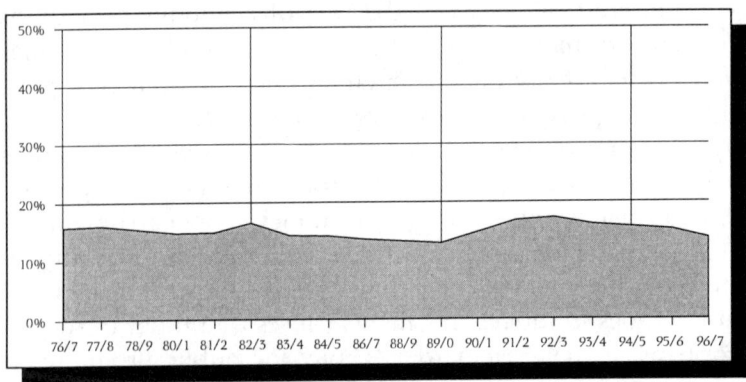

Source: Dominion Bond Rating Service, Nov. 1996.

In 1976, the ratio of program spending to Ontario's GDP was 15.9%. Since then it has ranged from a low of 13.6% in the late 1980s to a high of 17.3% in the recession of the 1990s. The average ratio of program spending as a percentage of the economy during the past twenty years was 15.3 %. For 1996–97, it is estimated at about 14%.

Program spending did not reach unusual levels relative to GDP during the 1989–94 recession. What is noteworthy about Ontario's fiscal situation during the recession of the 1990s was not the peak level of program spending relative to GDP, but the extreme nature of the change in the deficit that coincided with the recession and the length of time it has taken for economic recovery to bring down the ratio of program spending to GDP. The contrast with the 1981–83 period is particularly noteworthy. The Ontario economy recovered quite rapidly from that recession, and the recovery was reflected in an abrupt decline in the ratio of program spending to GDP. In the 1990s recession, however, recovery has been extremely slow and uneven. The relationship between Ontario's fiscal situation and the health of the economy is shown clearly in Figure 1.3.

Figure 1.3 Ontario's Program Spending as Percentage of Revenue, 1976–96

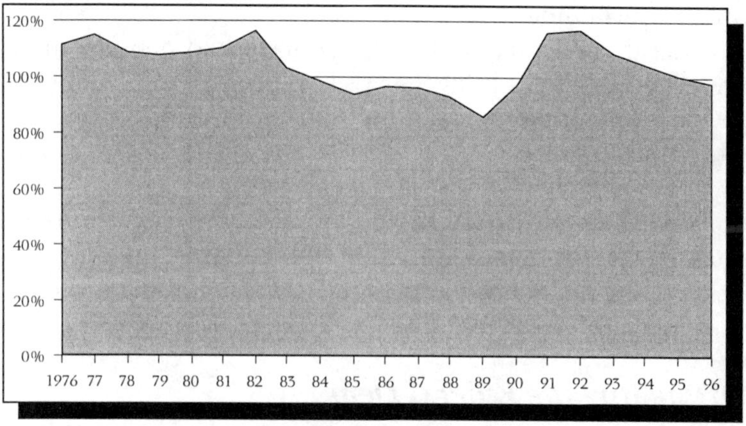

Source: Dominion Bond Rating Service, Nov. 1996

Ontario's spending, measured as a percentage of revenue, has fluctuated with economic activity in the province. Peaks in spending occur during recessions. The severity of the 1990 recession spread the spending peak over two fiscal years, 1990–91 and 1991–92.

What caused the Ontario debt to balloon in the 1990s was not some unprecedented increase in spending. Spending in the 1990s was consistent with spending during previous cyclical downturns. Rather, the debt was created primarily by the economic policies of the federal governments of Brian Mulroney and Jean Chrétien. These policies ignored the worsening problem of unemployment by imposing the most restrictive anti-inflationary policy in the industrialized world. Federal monetary and fiscal policies maintained cripplingly high real interest rates, which further reduced economic growth through the worst economic recession in Canada since the 1930s. The resulting unrealistically high exchange rate damaged Ontario's trading industries at the same time they were going through the wrenching adjustment to free trade. The economy has still not recovered from those disastrous policies: they have created a state of permanent recession. (Chapter 3, "Ontario's Jobs Crisis and Its Link to the Provincial Deficit," presents a more detailed discussion of employment in Ontario and its impact on provincial finances.)

Federal monetary and fiscal policies had a more direct impact on Ontario's budget as well. With respect to monetary policy, high interest rates increase borrowing costs. And when interest rates exceed the rate of growth of the economy, as they have for most of the period since the early 1980s, borrowing costs rise at an accelerating rate. When interest rates exceed the rate of growth in the economy, the only way to keep the deficit from increasing as a share of the economy is to increase taxes.

Offloading the Federal Debt

The federal government's decision to solve its fiscal problems largely on the backs of the provincial governments and the unemployed contributed further to Ontario's fiscal crisis.

A key factor behind Ontario's diminished fiscal capacity is the massive cutting of federal transfer payments to Ontario, which began slowly under Brian Mulroney in the mid-1980s and accelerated dramatically after the Liberals were elected in 1993. By 1998-99, Ontario will be receiving $2.8 billion less per year for health, education and welfare than it received in 1995-96. Billions more have already been chopped, as Ottawa's debt problems were simply offloaded onto the provinces. The kind of cooperative federalism that created Canada's social safety net has been abandoned.

On top of the federal transfer payment cuts, unemployment insurance has been gutted to such an extent that, in 1997, only one-third of Ontario's unemployed qualified for employment insurance, as opposed to two-thirds as recently as 1990 (see Figure 1.5). These changes have contributed directly to increased

Figure 1.4 Federal Transfers to Ontario, 1992–99

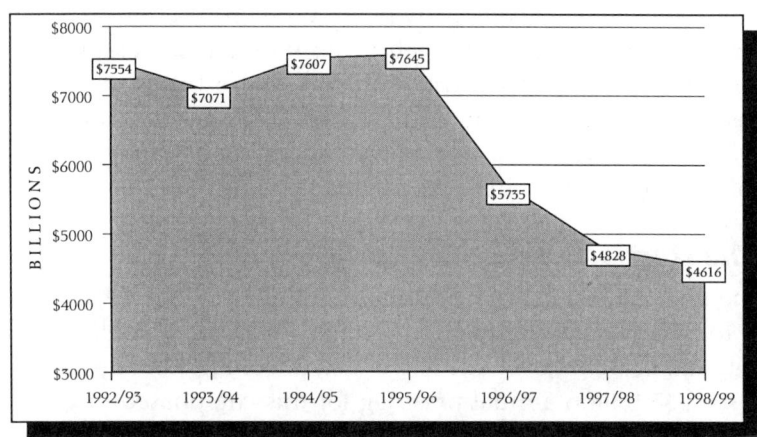

Figure 1.5 Federal Changes Push Jobless onto Welfare

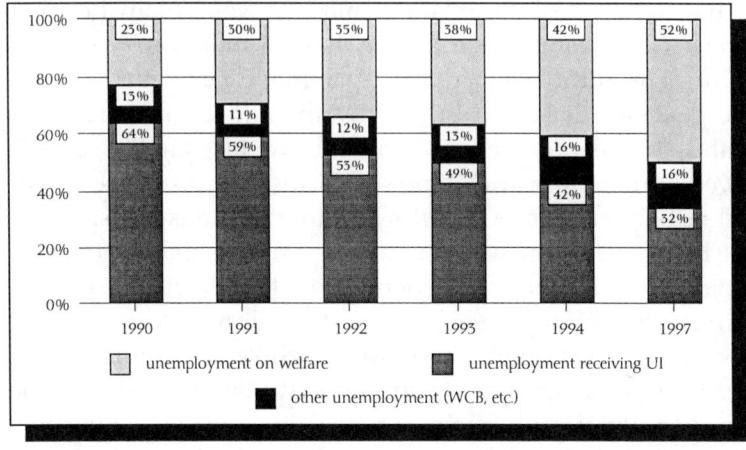

pressures on provincial spending during the recession.

Ottawa's failure to carry its fair share of the load helped to create Ontario's fiscal problems and continues to make a solution to those problems more difficult. The evidence makes it clear. Ontario does not have a spending problem, and never had. Ontario has a revenue problem – a fiscal capacity problem.

Despite that evidence, however, the Harris government has proceeded to hack away at vital public services in Ontario, all the while repeating its indefensible claim that spending is out of control and has to be brought down. Instead of attacking the real problem, the government has raised the stakes in its war against spending by reducing fiscal capacity still further through its tax cuts.

The Harris Tax Cut

The final cause underlying Ontario's diminished fiscal capacity is the Harris government's crowning folly: the $5 billion tax cut. The pre-election Common Sense Revolution booklet forecasts a $5 billion annual price tag for this cut, phased in gradually over four years and financed entirely by borrowing an additional $20 billion (all of which is added to the provincial debt). It remains to be seen what the final cost of this exercise in transferring cash to wealthy Ontarians will actually be; most likely it will climb much higher than $5 billion per year (see Figure 1.6). But it is already transparently clear that combining the goal of a balanced budget by the end of the millenium with a 30% cut in the provincial income tax rate has already severely undermined Ontario's capacity to support the essential public services required by a modern industrial state.

The irony, of course, as Figure 1.7 shows, is that for the vast majority of Ontarians the benefits of the Harris tax cut are minuscule. The top 20% of taxpayers will receive more than 50% of the total tax cut cash. Most people will be net losers, once user fees, service cuts and property tax hikes absorb the tax cut savings and much more besides. The mega-dumping of provincial costs onto municipal governments alone will cost the average Ontario family about $300.

One thing the tax cut does, however, is unmask the Harris Conservatives. The Common Sense Revolution is not about controlling spending – spending wasn't the cause of Ontario's fiscal problems in the first place. The Common Sense Revolution is not about fiscal responsibility. How can it be fiscally responsible to respond to a revenue crisis by

Figure 1.6 Annual Cost of Harris Tax Cut

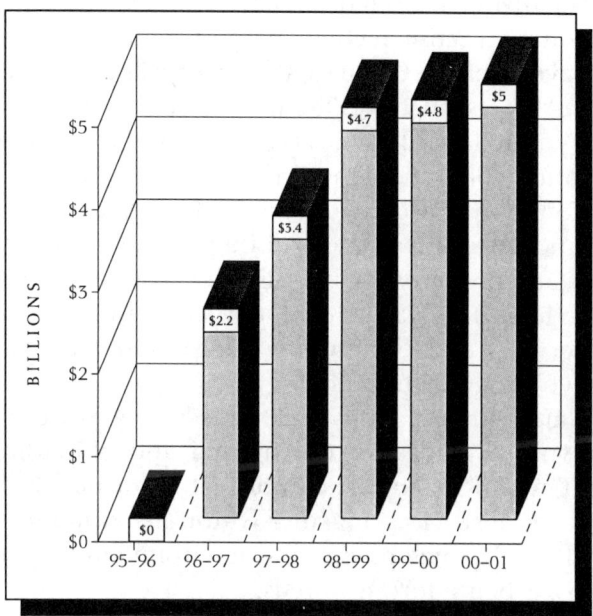

Figure 1.7 Tax Savings from Harris Tax Cut, by Income

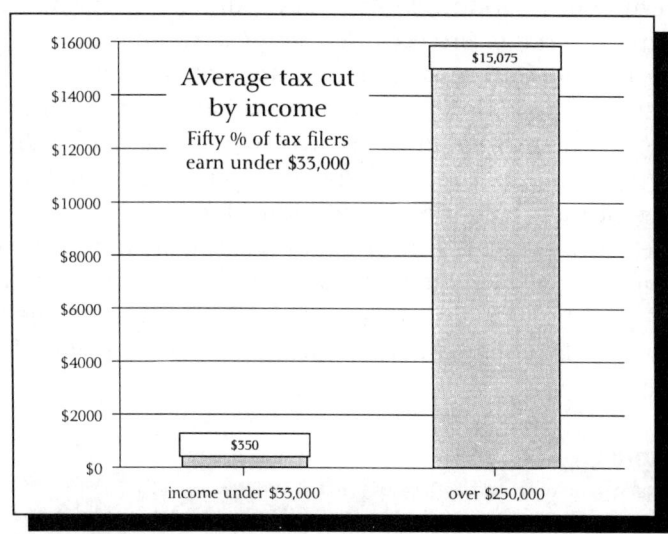

Source: Ernst & Young

cutting government revenues? What is fiscally responsible about borrowing $20 billion to pay for a tax cut?

The Common Sense Revolution is not about giving the average taxpayer a break. Ordinary Ontarians will get so little from the Harris tax cut that they'll barely notice it. And they'll pay every day in reduced health services, reduced access to education for their children, higher property taxes and user fees.

The Common Sense Revolution is about tax cuts for those who do not need them and will be paid for in service cuts, user fees and property tax increases by those who can afford them the least. The Harris revolution is about destroying the public services and community infrastructure that generations have struggled to build.

The Harris government's fiscal objectives have unleashed a whirlwind of cutbacks, downsizing and offloading that has left Ontario reeling. The entire fabric of health, education and social services, together with transportation, industrial and rural development and environmental protection programs, is being torn to shreds.

An Alternative

Government is about choices. One purpose of the Ontario Alternative Budget Project is to demonstrate that the choices made by the Harris government are not the only options available. The Working Group aims to identify and stimulate public discussion about alternative choices and to demonstrate that the choices made by the Harris government are wrong-headed, unfair and counterproductive.

There is a rational, humane and realistic alternative to the Common Sense Revolution, an alternative that solves the real fiscal problems facing this province, that builds on the achievements of the past and prepares a solid foundation for a better future.

Endnote

1 For a discussion of the relationship between high interest rates and a growing debt burden, see Jim Stanford, "Growth, Interest and Debt," in *The 1997 Alternative Budget* (Ottawa: Canadian Centre for Policy Alternatives/Laurier, 1997).

Chapter Two

OPTIONS FOR RESTORING ONTARIO'S FISCAL CAPACITY

This paper is intended to be a basis for the discussion of progressive options for dealing with Ontario's fiscal situation. It provides the following:

- An analysis of the current fiscal situation;
- A description of four different scenarios that balance the provincial budget and maintain or enhance public services in Ontario;
- A description of various tax policy options.

Analysis of current situation

Over the past 10 years, federal government policies have damaged Ontario's fiscal capacity. The federal government's policies of high unemployment, high interest rates and unconscionable tax give-aways for the highest-income Canadians along with massive cuts in federal programs like unemployment insurance have had an indirect impact. The unilateral termination of decades of cooperative federal-provincial financing of Canada's social programs has reduced Ontario's revenue directly. All of these policies have played a part in creating a near-crisis in Ontario's finances.

Conspicuously absent from the list of legitimate causes of Ontario's fiscal problems is Ontario's own program spending. The Harris government's mantra "out-of-control spending is the cause of Ontario's deficit" cannot obscure the fact that there is no evidence to support that claim. Saying it does not make it so.

Identifying the underlying causes of our current situation is helpful in understanding how we got here. But it does not solve the problems. We have real fiscal capacity problems. Blaming the federal government will not make them go away. Public debt interest now consumes over 20% of the total revenue of the Province of Ontario. The government is now taking in more revenue than it is spending on programs. Public debt interest payments account for the entire deficit. The provincial debt is now 32% of Gross Provincial Product. This is not sustainable over the long term, either economically or politically.

The level of public debt has a number of negative impacts. It places public services in jeopardy and undermines Ontarians confidence in the value of public services that they receive for their taxes. It also curtails the ability of the government to stabilize the economy during recessions and to respond to the changing needs of the community on an on-going basis.

Over the course of the economic cycle, from expansion to recession and back to expansion, the budget must be balanced.

In developing a menu of alternative scenarios to the Harris attack on Ontario, we are committed to balancing Ontario's budget over the same time horizon as originally set out in the so-called Common Sense Revolution. We are also committed to solving Ontario's fiscal capacity problems without sacrificing the public services that are so important to the quality of life in every community. Each of the alternative scenarios we have developed meets or exceeds these basic criteria. Each scenario, at a minimum, restores program resources to their levels before the Harris axe started to fall. And in each scenario, the budget balances within a year of the balance-year in the original Harris CSR scheme.

We present scenarios with quite different implications for the future of public services, employment growth and public revenues. Each scenario also makes a point about economic and social policy choices, both federally and provincially.

We put these scenarios forward to stimulate debate about the choices open to us for our future as a community.

The Harris scheme in detail

	Final 1995-96	Interim 1996-97	Budget 1997-98	Forecast From Common Sense Revolution 1998-99	1999-00	2000-01
Revenue	$48,359	$49,143	$48,400	$47,480	$49,690	$52,010
Program Spending	47,478*	45,598	44,557	41,410	41,410	41,410
Public Debt Interest	8,255	8,709	9,158	9,763	9,966	10,059
Reserve			650			
Restructuring Fund			610			
Non-Recurring Expenditures	1,352*	2,306				
Reported Surplus (Deficit)	(8,726)	(7,470)	(6,575)	(3,693)	(1,686)	541

Total Spending for 1995-96 = $48,830

Source: Dominion Bond Rating Service (DBRS), Ontario Finances, and the Common Sense Revolution

* Non-recurring expenditure = $520m employee severance, $128m to cancel social housing, $30m to cancel MPP pension plan, $30m to cancel Eglinton Subway, $400m early retirement pensions for OPS, $260m oil and gas tax refunds, $63m ODC loan losses. (Ontario Financing Report 1996. DBRS Nov/96)

Base Year Spending for 1995-96 consists of ($millions)

Program Spending	44,005
Capital	3,473
Subtotal	47,478
Restructuring	1,352
Total	48,830

Four points concerning this scheme should be considered.

- Harris proposed to reduce program spending from approximately $47.5 billion to $41.4 billion by 1999 – a drop of $6 billion or almost 13 percent.
- To date, although cuts in program spending of more than $5 billion have been announced; less than $2.0 billion in program spending cuts had actually taken effect by the end of 1996–7. And even that cut was more than offset by $2.3 billion in restructuring spending. We have only begun to feel the effects of the cuts.
- Even this level of spending cuts will not be able to pay for the tax cut. Over a five-year term of office, deficit-fighting Mike Harris will add $30 billion to the public debt, of which $20 billion will be directly attributable to the income tax and payroll tax cuts.
- Interest on the public debt will rise from 15% of total spending to 20%.

Alternative scenarios: common elements

At a minimum, the key features of the Harris tax cut and public service destruction scheme have to go. The income tax cut must be rescinded. And the decrease in Ontario's economic growth caused by Harris massive disinvestment in Ontario's future must be eliminated.

1. Cut the Tax Cut

The first step in restoring the capacity of Ontario's provincial and local governments to tackle the problems confronting us would be to abandon the foolish and destructive Harris tax cut. This would immediately restore $3 billion in revenue in 1997–98 and would avoid the loss of at least an additional $2 billion as the remainder of the tax cut is rolled out in future years. Over the next four years, it would save Ontario about $18 billion in lost revenue and interest charges. Using a tax cut to solve a fiscal problem is like digging downwards to get out of a hole. It just makes the problem bigger and more difficult and painful to solve.

2. *End the CSR Drag Effect:*
   restore investment in jobs and services
   The Common Sense Revolutionaries admitted in their pre-election booklet that the proposed spending cutbacks would have what economists call a drag effect on Ontario's economy. They conceded that the loss of over $8 billion in public investment and the loss of tens of thousands of jobs in the public sector would actually shrink Ontario's economy by 0.4% for each year they hold office. This means the loss of thousands more jobs in the private sector that depend on the spending of public employers and employees. It also means the loss of billions of dollars in public revenue. We estimate that wiping out the drag caused by the Harris spending cuts would generate an additional $1 billion in revenue by 2001-2.

From this common base, we have developed four scenarios.

- In scenario one, program spending remains at its 1995-6 level.

- In scenario two, program spending increases from that base at a rate sufficient to keep real per capita program spending constant. This means that spending per person, adjusted for inflation, is unchanged.

- Scenario three has program spending increasing to its share of the Ontario economy in 1989-90 (the last year in which we had close to full employment in this province, or 13.75%) and then maintained at that share.

- Scenario four has spending increasing at the same rate as in scenario two, maintaining real per capita spending at the 1995-6 level, but assumes a federal commitment to employment and to cooperative federal-provincial funding of major social programs.

Scenario one – flatline spending

This scenario maintains public spending at its 1995–6 level. Economic growth is based on the forecast for Ontario of the widely respected economic forecaster Informetrica and is in line with estimates from other private sector forecasters. In addition, we assume that growth will be 0.4% faster as the CSR drag is eliminated. This is based on estimates of the drag itself presented in the Common Sense Revolution.

In this scenario, provincial revenue is about $7.5 billion higher than that projected by the Dominion Bond Rating Service (DBRS) for the Harris plan for 2000–1. $5.5 billion of this amount comes from eliminating the tax cut, $1.0 billion comes from economic growth restored by the elimination of the CSR drag and $1.0 billion comes from higher-than-expected growth in 1995–6 and 1996–7 and the impact of growth on the cost of the tax cut. Public services spending exceeds the DBRS projection by $6 billion. By fiscal year 2000–1, there is an overall surplus of $2.9 billion.

Compared with the base year of 1995–6, revenue is $11.2 billion higher, all of which is attributable to economic growth.

This scenario demonstrates clearly that the Harris fiscal crisis is in fact a crisis created by the Harris scheme itself. With no tax increases at all, this scenario produces a surplus by the end of Harris first term.

The freeze in nominal spending at 1995–6 levels in this scenario avoids the vicious bloodletting of the Harris scheme. But it constrains significantly the ability of Ontario's public services system to meet our needs in the face of higher costs due to inflation and a growing population. By the year 2000–1 in this scenario, total public spending as a percentage of GDP will have dropped to 13%. Program spending will be 10.5%, compared with the average over the 1980s of 15%.

Scenario 1 – flatline

($ millions)	Harris 1997–98	1997–98	1998–99	1999–00	2000–01
Revenue	$48,400	$52,327	$54,312	$56,817	$59,450
Program Spending	45,819	47,773	47,573	47,573	47,573
Public Debt Interest	9,158	9,014	9,136	9,113	8,946
Surplus (deficit)	(6,575)	(4,459)	(2,397)	130	2,931
Increase over Harris expenditure		1,951	6,113	6,113	6,113

Key Assumptions	1997–98	1998–99	1999–00	2000–01	2001–02
Real Growth	3.7%	3.8%	3.2%	3.2%	3.0%
Inflation	1.7%	1.8%	1.8%	1.8%	1.8%
Interest Rates	6%	5.5%	5.5%	5.5%	5.5%
CSR drag	.4%	.4%	.4%	.4%	0%

Scenario two – constant real per capita spending

In this scenario, program spending increases enough to maintain constant real per capita spending. By 2001-2, public services spending is $8 billion higher than in the flatline scenario; nearly $14 billion higher than in the DBRS projection.

The difference in the quality and level of public services in Ontario in this scenario compared with the Harris scheme is profound. Investment in public services is roughly 33% higher by 2001-2. But these increases only maintain the real level of per-capita service we had in 1995-6. This underlines how dramatically impoverished public services will be in Ontario by the year 2001-2.

There is a budgetary surplus of more than $750 million by 2001-2.

Of the $16.7 billion in revenue growth from the 1995-6 base that achieves this result, $15 billion comes from economic growth and $1.7 billion (1997-8 base) from the introduction of a fair tax package.

Compared with the Harris scheme, this scenario raises an additional $11.1 billion by fiscal year 2001-2, of which $5.5

billion comes from eliminating the tax cut, $2.7 billion from the fair tax package, and $3.9 billion from higher-than-expected growth in 1996-7, the impact of growth on the cost of the Harris tax cut, additional economic growth arising from the elimination of the CSR drag and the additional spending at a constant real per capita level.

Scenario 2 – constant real per capita spending

($ millions)	1997-98	1998-99	1999-00	2000-01	2001-02
Revenue	$54,149	$56,381	$59,255	$62,291	$65,084
Program Spending	51,351	51,149	52,484	53,857	55,267
Public Debt Interest	9,014	9,232	9,298	9,277	9,031
Surplus (Deficit)	(6,216)	(4,000)	(2,527)	(842)	786
Increase over Harris expenditure	8,051	9,739	11,074	12,447	13,857
Key Assumptions	1997-98	1998-99	1999-00	2000-01	2001-02
Real Growth	4%	4.3%	3.7%	3.7%	3%

Scenario three – maintain the provincial public sector at 1989-90 share of economy

In this scenario, public spending increases from the 1995-6 base until it reaches the 1989-90 share of the economy of 13.75%, and then maintains that share. Program spending reaches $58 billion by 2001-2, $16.5 billion or roughly 40% higher than the DBRS projection for the CSR.

This scenario highlights how dramatically the Harris scheme shrinks the public economy. Relative to the size of the economy, Harris public services will be reduced by one quarter by the year 2001-2. One quarter less investment in our economic future. One quarter less of a commitment to the least fortunate in our society. One quarter less directed to the public services that make the quality of life in Ontario what it is today.

It also highlights how substantially our fiscal capacity has been diminished by the actions of the federal government.

To balance the budget and maintain the Ontario public service share of the total economy, $3.3 billion in new taxes would be required by the year 2001–2. The remaining $9.6 billion in increased revenue, compared with the Harris scheme, would result from eliminating the Harris income tax cut and additional economic growth.

Scenario 3 – maintain spending at 1989-90 share of economy

($ millions)	PLAN 3 1997–98	1998–99	1999–00	2000–01	2001–02
Revenue	$55,727	$57,959	$60,920	$64,047	$66,924
Program Spending	51,351	52,149	52,484	55,239	57,891
Public Debt Interest	9,014	9,146	9,175	9,055	8,777
Surplus (Deficit)	(4,638)	(3,336)	(739)	(247)	257
Increase over Harris expenditure	8,051	10,739	11,074	13,829	16,481
Key Assumptions	1997–98	1998–99	1999–00	2000–01	2001–02
Real Growth	4%	4.3%	3.7%	3.7%	3.0%

Scenario four – national employment targets and a commitment to cooperative federalism

The first three scenarios do not assume any change from the stagnation-inducing policies of the federal government. National economic policy remains fixated on unrealistic inflation targets and the federal government's retreat from federal-provincial funding partnerships continues.

The size of the tax package needed to maintain public services' share of the Ontario economy, illustrated by scenario 3, highlights that impact.

Scenario four paints the picture in even sharper relief.

Now in it's third year, Canada's Alternative Federal Budget has demonstrated that there is a practical, realistic and doable choice that lets us escape from the treadmill of recession-making federal budgets.

Ontario's budget making does not take place in a vacuum. That is why it is important to demonstrate, in at least one fiscal scenario, how dramatically Ontario's fiscal situation would be enhanced if the measures outlined in Canada's Alternate Federal Budget were put into effect. The major beneficial impacts for Ontario would be three-fold.

First, a return to fair share policies by a Government of Canada would restore transfer payments for health, education and welfare to 1995 levels, as proposed in this years Alternative Federal Budget. New transfer payments to Ontario from the AFB's Social Investment Funds would total $2.1 billion for 1997–98.

Second, because Ontario income tax revenue is linked to federal income tax revenue, Ontario's revenue from personal income taxes would increase as a result of the AFB measures to restrict capital gains exemptions and create new tax brackets for individuals with incomes over $100,000 a year. On a 1995–6 base, that would add about $700 million to Ontario's revenue.

Third, the growth-promoting policies of the Alternative Federal Budget would generate additional growth in Ontario's economy.

These factors, combined with the impact on Ontario of eliminating the CSR drag would allow the province to maintain real per capita spending with no tax increase (instead of the $1.7 billion increase required by scenario two) and still produce a surplus of $447 million by the year 1999–2000 ($5.6 billion by 2001–2).

Scenario 4 – national commitment to growth and cooperative federal-provincial funding

($ millions)	1997–98	1998–99	1999–00	2000–01	2001–02
Revenue	$55,851	$59,356	$63,328	$67,606	$71,777
Program Spending	51,667	51,941	53,783	55,695	57,679
Public Debt Interest	9,014	9,156	9,097	8,913	8,456

($ millions)	1997–98	1998–99	1999–00	2000–01	2001–02
Surplus (Deficit)	(4,830)	(1,742)	447	2,998	5,642
Increase over Harris expenditure	8,367	10,531	12,373	14,285	16,269
Key Assumptions	1997–98	1998–99	1999–00	2000–01	2001–02
Real Growth	4.8%	5.3%	4.7%	4.7%	4.0%
Inflation	2.4%	2.8%	2.8%	2.8%	2.8%

The building blocks

1. Economic Growth

The starting point for each of the scenarios is the forecast for economic growth in Ontario in the base case forecast of Informetrica, which in turn follows closely the consensus of other private sector forecasts. From that base, adjustments are made for each scenario based on the estimated impact of the fiscal position projected in the scenario.

These projections of GDP growth are:

1996–7	1.9%
1997–8	3.3%
1998–9	3.4%
1999–2000	2.8%
2000–1	2.8%
2001–2	3.0%

In the "flatline spending" scenario, the fiscal stimulus consists of the reversal of $6 billion net in spending cuts in the Common Sense Revolution. The authors of the Common Sense Revolution themselves estimated that the "fiscal drag" from those cuts would reduce growth by 0.4% in each year of their mandate. Scenario one increases growth rate projections by that amount to reflect the impact of eliminating those cuts.

In the "maintain real per capita spending" scenario, the fiscal stimulus consists of the $6 bilion noted above plus an additional $8 billion to maintain constant real per capita spending by the fiscal year 2000–1. This is offset in part by the projected

$2.7 billion in tax increases required to balance the budget by the year 2000-1. We estimate that this additional stimulus will increase projected growth by a further 0.25% in the first year, and 0.5% in the second, third and fourth years.

In the most expansive scenario, the "maintain the 1989-90 share of economy" scenario, the stimulus from spending is higher than scenario two by approximately $2.6 billion. This is offset in part by the impact of the projected $1.9 billion increase in taxes required to balance the budget by the year 2000-1.

Scenario four maintains the Ontario level stimulus of the "maintain real per capita spending" scenario two. Where it differs from that scenario, however, is in taking into account the impact on economic growth of the commitment to employment and growth reflected in the Alternative Federal Budget proposals. The AFB projects ongoing additional growth reaching 2%, divided evenly between additional real growth and slightly higher inflation – 2.8% as opposed to the forecast of 1.8%.

2. A Fair Tax Package

The choices to be made in developing a fair tax policy in Ontario are not easy. As a provincial government, Ontario must deal with constitutional, institutional and practical economic limitations on its ability raise revenue. Choices must be considered which, were these limitations not present, would be rejected as second-best options. In particular, these limitations constrain options with respect to corporate taxation, taxation of income from capital and wealth taxation. Substantial changes in these areas could only realistically be accomplished in the context of a truly national effort at fair tax reform. Only in the AFB scenario are we able to take these kinds of changes into account.

The goal of fair tax policy cannot be pursued in isolation from other public policy goals. In particular, we must have the fiscal capacity to support the public services we need. And in achieving a balance between these two goals, we must recognize that public services themselves redistribute income.

Revenue sources

As a Provincial Government, Ontario has a limited range of options to raise more tax revenue. Ontario operates under the rules of the Federal tax laws and is subject to the loopholes, exemptions, write-offs and deductions which allow corporations and the wealthy to escape paying their fair share. At the end of the day the kind of reform proposed in the Alternative Federal Budget are essential.

But there are measures which Ontario can take to reinforce its fiscal capacity. Here is a list of possible options.

- **Personal Income Tax**

    In 1996-7, the personal income tax raises approximately $16.4 billion (taking into account the $1.2 billion announced cost of the Harris tax cut.)

    A 1% increase in provincial income tax from the normal level of $17.6 billion would raise $176 million.

- **Retail Sales Tax — rate**

    In 1996-7, the retail sales tax raises approximately $9.8 billion.

    The Ontario retail sales tax rate is 8%. Each point raises $1.21 billion

- **Retail Sales Tax — base**

    There are various options for broadening the base of the retail sales tax. A number of those options would extend the sales tax to services that are primarily consumed by business and to financial services that are exempt from the GST.

Air transportation	$346 million
Railway transport	$178 million
Truck transport	$481 million
Legal, accounting services	$334 million
Financial services excl. real estate	$568 million
Aviation fuel	$ 28 million

- **Corporate Income Tax**

    In 1996–7, corporate income and capital taxes raise $5.7 billion.

    The general rate is 14.5%. Each point raises $400 million. Small business corporations pay a preferred rate of 10%. Eliminating the preferred rate raises $535 million.
    Ending deductions for meals and entertainment raises $66 million
    Ending preferred treatment for manufacturing and processing raises $88 million

- **Tobacco Tax**

    Tobacco taxes raised $350 million in 1995–6.

    Rates were partially restored to the levels of the early 1990s this year.
    A full restoration would raise $400 million.

- **Employer Health Tax**

    The employer health tax raises a total of $2.7 billion in 1996–7.

    The rate of tax is on a sliding scale from 0, for payrolls below $200,000 to 1.95% for payrolls above $400,000.

    Each 0.1% yields $150 million.

    Restoring the payroll tax to the 0.95% to 1.95% scale that existed until the 1996–7 budget would raise an estimated $150 million.

    Moving to a flat 1.95% tax would raise an estimated $260 million.

The other major sources of tax revenue are Gasoline and Motor Vehicle Fuel Taxes ($2.5 billion in 1996–7) and Land Transfer Tax ($435 million in 1996–7).

Options for paying for public services

In scenarios one and four, no new taxes are required. In scenario four, the AFB scenario, income tax revenue increases by an estimated $700 million because of changes to the federal income tax base and rates that would be reflected in Ontario income tax revenue potential.

In scenario two – maintaining real per capita spending, $1.7 billion must be raised in new taxes.

That amount could be raised, for example, by broadening the base of the retail sales tax to include legal and accounting services and financial services ($902 million); making the EHT a flat tax at 1.95%; and restoring tobacco taxation to its early-1990s level ($400 million).

Scenario three – maintaining Ontario spending as a share of the economy with 1989–90 as the base – would require a larger increase in tax revenue – $1.5 billion higher than the amount required in scenario two, or a total of just over $3.2 billion. For example, an increase of three points of corporate tax would raise an additional $1.2 billion; extending the retail sales tax further to include air transportation would raise $350 million.

3. Transfers from the Federal Government

The effort to restore Ontario's fiscal capacity needs to take into account the effect of more than a decade of actions by the Government of Canada to dump it's debt problem onto the shoulders of the provinces, especially Ontario's.

All scenarios except scenario four assume Federal Government transfers will continue to decline as set out in various Federal budget statements. The assumed amounts are:

1995–6	$7,645 million
1996–7	$5.735 million, a cut of $1.9 billion.
1997–8	$4,828 million, a further cut of $900 million.
1998–9	$4,616 million, a further cut of $200 million.

In the AFB/cooperative federalism scenario, these numbers are dramatically different, because they reflect a renewed commitment to federal/provincial funding of education, health and social services as reflected in the 1997–8 Alternative Federal Budget.

Total transfers in that scenario are increased by $2,061 million in 1997–8 from the projected level of $4,828 million for 1997–8 and maintained at that level throughout.

Summary comparison of scenarios

The following charts summarize the four scenarios as compared with the Harris scheme with respect to revenue, total spending, new taxes and deficit.

Figure 2.1 Alternative Scenarios vs Harris Scheme: Revenue

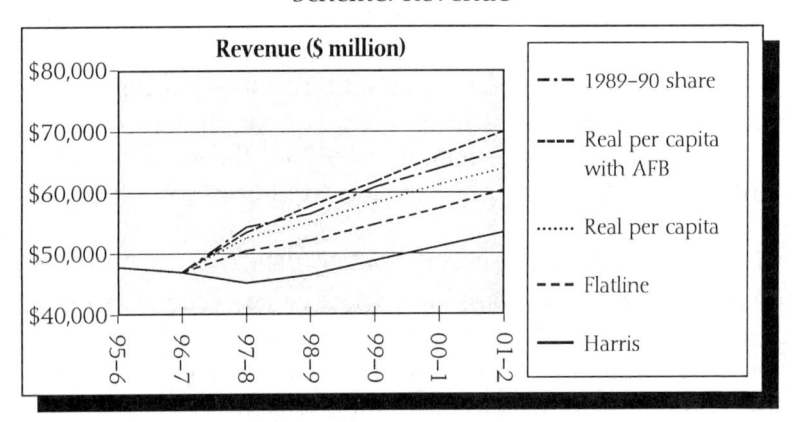

Figure 2.2 Alternative Scenarios vs Harris Scheme: Program Expenditures

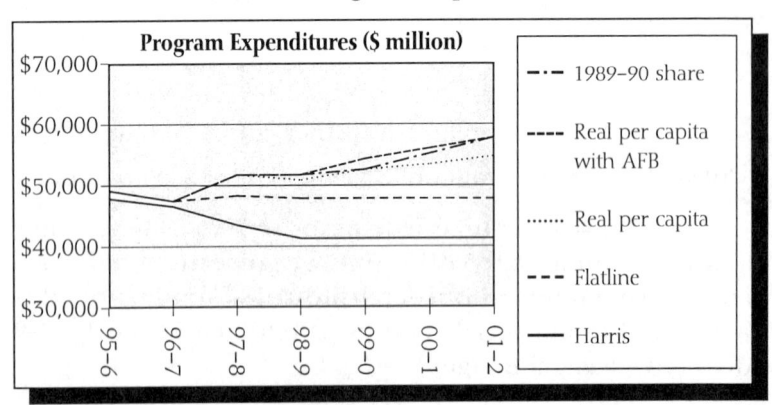

Figure 2.3 Alternative Scenarios vs Harris Scheme: New Taxes

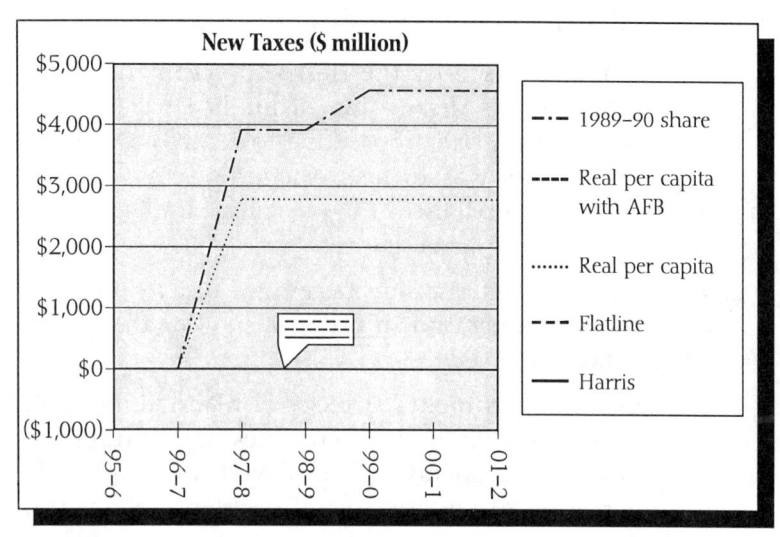

New Taxes ($ million), 1995–6 to 2001–2
- –·– 1989–90 share
- ---- Real per capita with AFB
- ······ Real per capita
- --- Flatline
- —— Harris

Figure 2.4 Alternative Scenarios vs Harris Scheme: Deficit

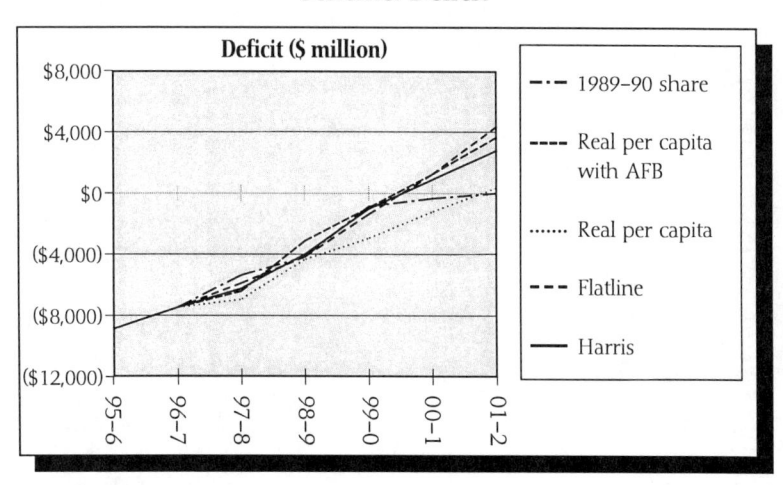

Deficit ($ million), 1995–6 to 2001–2
- –·– 1989–90 share
- ---- Real per capita with AFB
- ······ Real per capita
- --- Flatline
- —— Harris

These scenarios all achieve essentially the same deficit result as the Harris scheme, but with dramatically different outcomes for public services in the province.

While these scenarios are presented as a focus for discussion of Ontario's fiscal options, there are some conclusions that can be drawn from the exercise at this level.

1. The fiscal crisis used by the Harris Government as the justification for its decimation of public services does not exist. All that had to be done to remedy Ontario's deficit in 1995–6 was to keep spending constant. The flat line scenario balances the provincial budget in the same year as the Harris scheme.

2. The Harris budget cuts are necessary, not in order to balance the budget, but in order to pay for the Harris income tax cut.

3. The federal government's strategy of maintaining high real interest and unemployment rates and cutting the deficit by cutting spending has played the major role in the creation of Ontario's fiscal problems; a reversal of those policies would enable per capita real spending to be maintained with no tax increases.

Part II

Fighting the Jobs Deficit

Chapter Three

ONTARIO'S JOB CRISIS AND ITS LINK TO THE PROVINCIAL DEFICIT

The Unemployment Rate: Just the Tip of the Iceberg

For more than six years, starting in 1991, the provincial unemployment rate has averaged almost 10% (see Figure 3.1). As of April 1997, the province's unemployment rate still stood at 9% – an increase of 0.3 points since the election of the Harris government in June 1995.

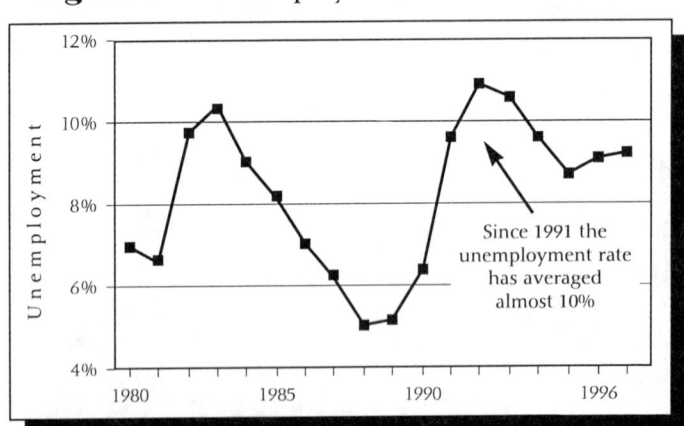

Figure 3.1 Unemployment in Ontario, 1980–97

Since 1991 the unemployment rate has averaged almost 10%

This is by far the longest period of sustained high unemployment in the province since the 1930s. In contrast, during the recession of the early 1980s (which was more severe than the recession of 1990–1992 in terms of the proportionate decline in output), the provincial unemployment rate exceeded 9% for just two years. Five years after reaching the bottom of that recession, provincial unemployment had declined to 5%. Five years after the bottom of the 1990–92 recession, on the other hand, unemployment still exceeds 9%.

The Real Extent of Unemployment in Ontario

As bad as the official unemployment numbers are, they only partially describe the true extent of the job crisis in Ontario. The official unemployment tally includes only those unemployed workers who meet the Statistics Canada definition of actively looking for work, and not those Ontarians so discouraged by the depressed labour market that they have given up a sufficiently active job search to count as officially unemployed. These individuals appear in the statistics as having left the labour force altogether. Nevertheless, they represent a pool of unutilized labour potential, and for all intents and purposes, they should be counted among unemployed.

Figure 3.2 Labour Force Participation in Ontario, 1980–97

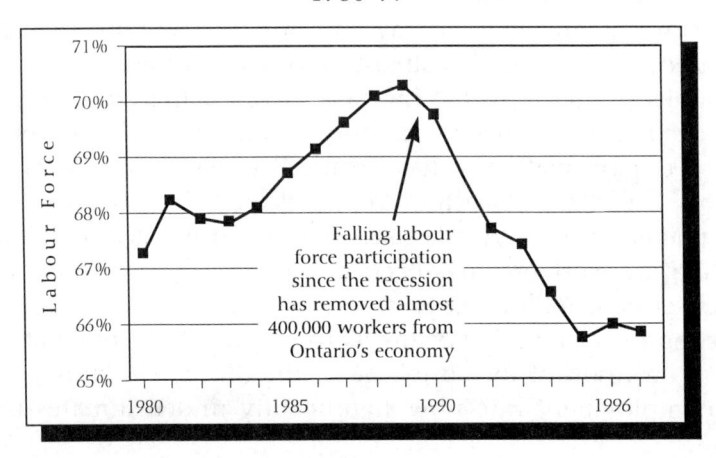

Falling labour force participation since the recession has removed almost 400,000 workers from Ontario's economy

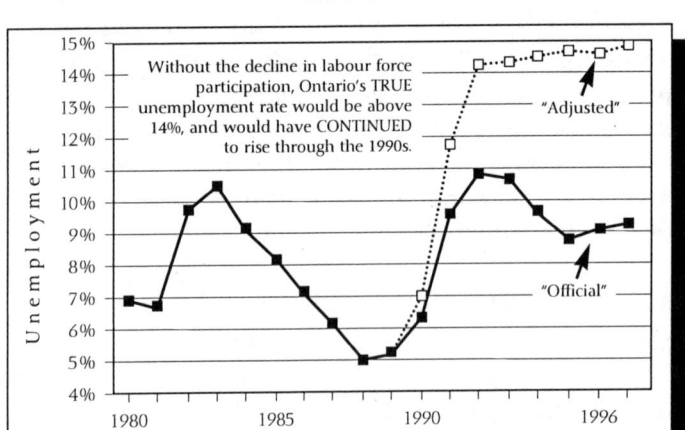

Figure 3.3 Unemployment: Official and Adjusted, 1980–97

Without the decline in labour force participation, Ontario's TRUE unemployment rate would be above 14%, and would have CONTINUED to rise through the 1990s.

As illustrated in Figure 3.2, labour force participation in Ontario has plunged since the last recession, precisely because of prolonged, depressed labour market conditions. Participation by working age Ontarians fell steadily from a peak of over 70% in 1989 to less than 66% by 1995, where it has languished since. If labour force participation had remained at its pre-recession levels, some 400,000 additional Ontarians would be active in the provincial labour market (working or looking for work). This decline in labour force participation represents a huge step backwards for our economy and our society: prior to 1989, participation had grown almost every year for thirty-five years, thanks primarily to the increased work activity of women. Indeed, had that previous historical trend continued, we would expect participation to have reached levels close to 75% by now. If anything, the actual drop in the participation rate (some 4 points since 1989) understates both the true extent to which Ontario's workforce has been ravaged by the recession and subsequent jobless recovery and the degree to which our economy is operating below its true productive potential.

As a result of the shrinkage of the official workforce, the unemployment rate now significantly underestimates the true problem of unemployment in Ontario. This is illustrated in Figure 3.3, which compares the official unemployment rate with the unemployment rate that would have been experienced had labour force participation stayed constant at its pre-recession peak. When the discouraged workers who have abandoned Ontario's job market during the 1990s are added to the unemployment tally, true unemployment in the province would have exceeded 14% since 1992. What is worse, there would have been no improvement in that true unemployment rate since the bottom of the last recession; in fact, the unemployment rate would actually have continued to slowly increase. This suggests that even the modest decline in official unemployment that has been experienced in Ontario since 1991 (from 11 to 9%) has been due exclusively and perversely to the decline in labour force participation (rather than to the creation of new jobs).

Figure 3.4 provides a different perspective on the same grim landscape. Turn the unemployment rate upside down and we have what economists call the employment rate: that is, the proportion of working-age Ontarians actually employed at a given time. This measure sidesteps the need to make a distinction between workers who are out of work but actively seeking jobs (thus officially qualifying as unemployed) and those who have simply abandoned the labour market altogether. The employment rate is now a more accurate measure of the jobs crisis in Canada in the 1990s because of the unprecedented growth of the number of discouraged workers. Ontario's employment rate plunged from 67% prior to the recession to just 60% three years later. And the employment rate has not increased in the five years since then.

No wonder that so many Ontarians have felt that our economic recovery (now in its sixth consecutive year) has, in fact, not been a recovery at all. Indeed, from the perspective of the labour market, there has been no recovery. And it is not surprising that Ontario's public finances (which were roughly in balance prior to the recession) fell apart so dramatically in the early 1990s: a full 7% of the entire working-age population that had been working and paying taxes prior to 1990 has no longer been doing so throughout this depressed decade. To get Ontario's employment rate back to its pre-recession levels requires creating and filling of 600,000 additional jobs. On top of the huge economic and social benefits that would result from this sea change in our provincial labour market, the massive and automatic benefits to provincial finances of a return to a high-employment economy would play a key role in a progressive solution to our deficit and debt problems.

Figure 3.4 Ontario's Falling Employment Rate, 1985–97

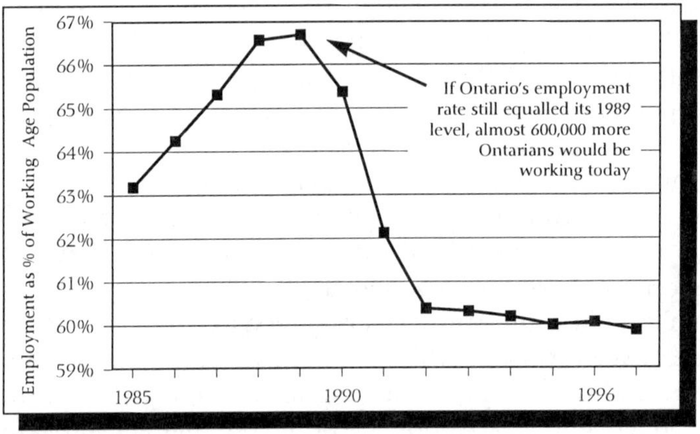

[Chart: Employment as % of Working Age Population, ranging from 59% to 67%, 1985–1996. Annotation: "If Ontario's employment rate still equalled its 1989 level, almost 600,000 more Ontarians would be working today"]

The Youth Unemployment Ghetto

Ontario's official youth unemployment rate in January 1997 was 16.8% which was close to twice the rate for the population as a whole. As well, the problems of hidden unemployment and discouraged workers are even more severe for young people than for the population at large. For example, as illustrated in Figure 3.5, labour force participation for Ontario workers aged fifteen to twenty-four has declined from a peak of 74% before the recession to just 62% in 1997. Young people used to be more likely than the population at large to participate in the labour market; now they are significantly less likely to do so. One of every six young workers who participated in Ontario's labour market before the recession has since given up looking for work altogether.

Figure 3.5 Youth Force Participation, 1980–96

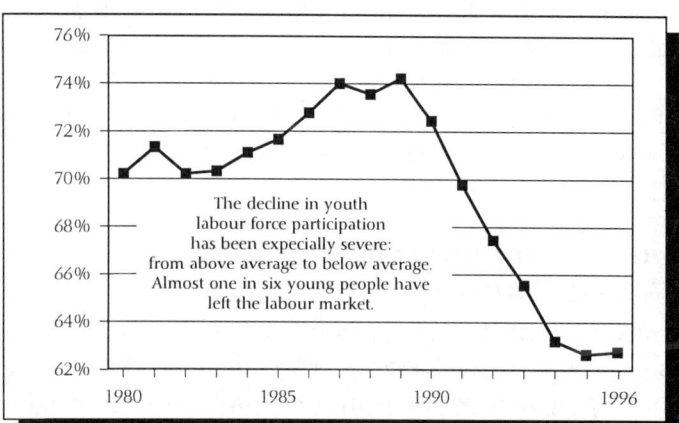

The decline in youth labour force participation has been expecially severe: from above average to below average. Almost one in six young people have left the labour market.

Figure 3.6 Youth Unemployment: Official and Adjusted, 1980–96

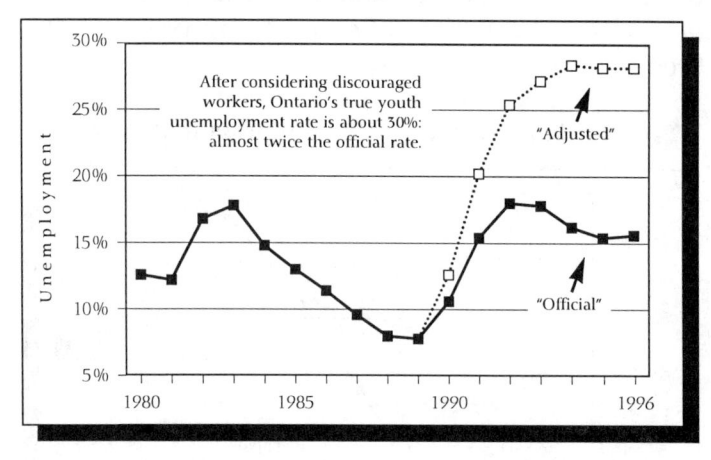

After considering discouraged workers, Ontario's true youth unemployment rate is about 30%: almost twice the official rate.

This state of affairs implies that the true unemployment crisis facing Ontario's youth is far worse than the official statistics suggest, as indicated in Figure 3.6. The unemployment rate that would prevail had youth labour force participation stayed at its pre-recession levels would be almost twice as high as the official rate, close to 30%. It is no exaggeration to state that young people in Ontario face a jobs crisis that rivals that of the 1930s. Some of this hidden unemployment has been absorbed in higher enrolment rates at post-secondary educational institutions. But given the uncertain job prospects that await new graduates and the growing financial barriers to post-secondary studies in this province, going back to university or college is clearly no permanent solution to this crisis.

Chronic Unemployment, Insecurity and Social Cutbacks

Not only has the unemployment rate remained extremely and stubbornly high (especially when the true extent of hidden unemployment is taken into account), but the length of time it typically takes an unemployed worker to find a new job has also increased substantially. As shown in Figure 3.7, the average duration of unemployment in Ontario more than doubled following the recession, from just thirteen weeks in 1989 to more than twenty-seven weeks by 1994. In 1997 the figures were only slightly lower.

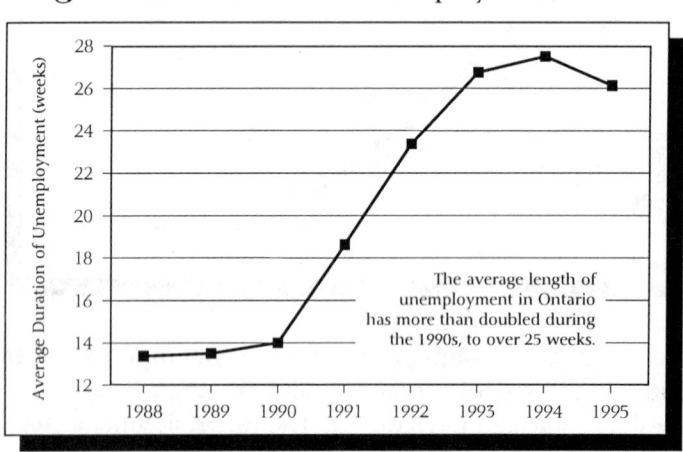

Figure 3.7 Duration of Unemployment, 1988–95

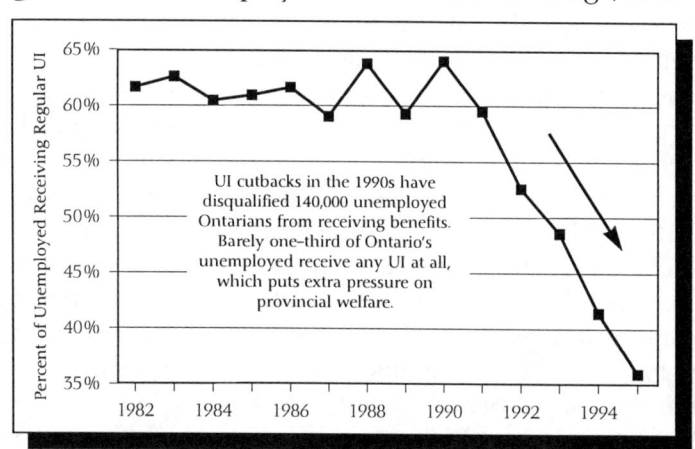

Figure 3.8 Unemployment Insurance Coverage, 1982–95

Chart: Percent of Unemployed Receiving Regular UI, 1982–1994. Values range from about 62% in the early 1980s, fluctuating between 55–62% through the late 1980s, then declining sharply in the 1990s to below 35% by 1994.

Chart annotation: UI cutbacks in the 1990s have disqualified 140,000 unemployed Ontarians from receiving benefits. Barely one-third of Ontario's unemployed receive any UI at all, which puts extra pressure on provincial welfare.

Because of both the high rate and the long duration of unemployment, the financial burden facing workers who lose their jobs has grown dramatically. Yet just when workers face the most precarious job market in sixty years, the social programs that were designed to alleviate their economic insecurity have been downsized dramatically. Nowhere is this more evident than in the case of Canada's unemployment insurance (or employment insurance) program. Thanks to cutbacks by successive Conservative and Liberal federal governments, it has become substantially more difficult for unemployed workers in Ontario to qualify for UI benefits (due to stricter qualifying requirements, shorter durations of benefits, and other changes). As a direct result, the proportion of Ontario's officially unemployed who qualify to receive any UI benefits has plunged from roughly 60–65% (typical levels prior to 1991), to less than 35% in 1995 (see Figure 3.8). In other words, two of three unemployed Ontarians used to qualify to receive UI, but this ratio has since fallen to just one in three. And this grim finding excludes those discouraged workers who don't show up in the official unemployment statistics, let alone qualify to receive unemployment benefits. Tens of thousands of these disqualified unemployed workers eventually showed up on

Ontario's welfare rolls. As discussed in Chapter 1, this federal dumping has been one of the main factors that pushed up provincial social assistance caseloads in the early 1990s.

The combination of persistent unemployment and rapidly disappearing social protection programs has produced an unprecedented economic insecurity for workers in Ontario, even for those lucky enough to have kept their jobs during the 1990s. This insecurity can be measured in the following fashion. The approximate "cost of job loss" for workers (that is, the out-of-pocket financial loss they suffer as a result of becoming unemployed) depends on two important factors: how long it takes them to find a new job and how much they will receive in UI benefits while they are looking.

Since the length of job search has grown while the likelihood of receiving UI has fallen by one-half, the total cost of job loss facing Ontario workers has increased dramatically. As illustrated in Figure 3.9, prior to the last recession workers in Ontario stood to lose about nine weeks of pay (net of UI benefits) if they lost their job. Today that figure is closer to twenty-two weeks of pay, enough to make most workers worry about losing their mortgages or their cars.[1]

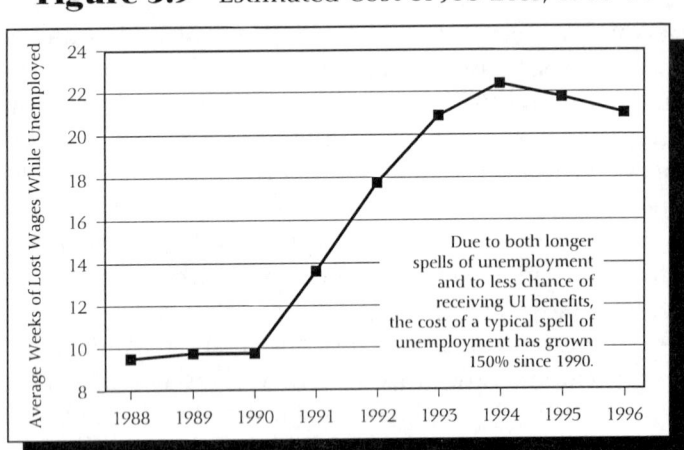

Figure 3.9 Estimated Cost of Job Loss, 1988–96

Due to both longer spells of unemployment and to less chance of receiving UI benefits, the cost of a typical spell of unemployment has grown 150% since 1990.

Little wonder that the mood of Ontario's labour market has changed, with the balance of bargaining power shifting so dramatically in favour of employers. Rather than demanding wage increases to reflect inflation and rising productivity, many workers now count themselves lucky to have a job at all.

The Clear-Cutting of Public Sector Employment

Ontario's general labour market conditions have been incredibly weak during the 1990s. But the sharp cutbacks in employment in Ontario's broader public sector that have been experienced, most dramatically since 1995, have only added to the malaise. In just the first year following the implementation of the initial spending cutbacks of the Harris government in the autumn of 1995, some 32,500 jobs disappeared from Ontario's public sector. Most of these job losses were experienced in the health care, social services, and education sectors. On top of the decline in service experienced by consumers of these publicly-supported programs, the economic costs of public sector layoffs have been severe. Without these public sector lay-offs, Ontario's lacklustre job-creation record since the Harris government was elected (only 61,000 jobs were created in Ontario between June 1995 and February 1997) would have been half-again as strong. The final impact of the public sector cutbacks is even larger than this, since many *private-sector* jobs, which are dependent on the spin-off spending power of public employees, have also been eliminated. Since the biggest spending cutbacks have yet to be fully experienced by labour-intensive public service providers (such as schools, hospitals, and social service agencies), the rollback of government in the Ontario economy that began in 1995 will continue to undermine our overall provincial job creation record.

False Solutions Part I: Competitiveness and Profits

Supporters of the Harris government's cutbacks seldom admit to the direct public-sector job losses that are the inevitable result of reduced spending. But even when these conse-

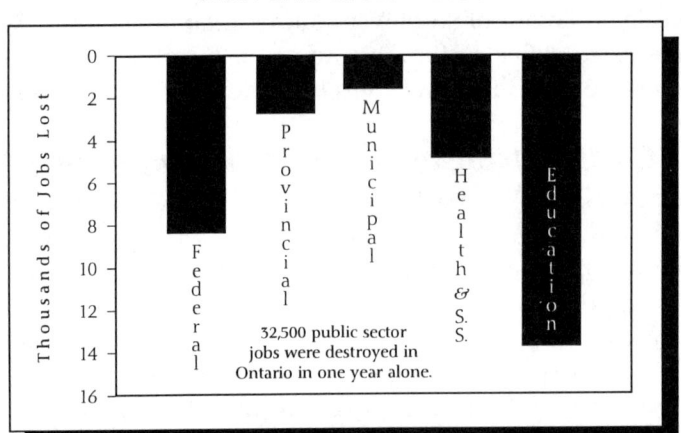

Figure 3.10 Public Sector Job Losses in Ontario, Nov. 1995 to Nov. 1996

32,500 public sector jobs were destroyed in Ontario in one year alone.

quences are recognized, it is argued that strong growth in the *private-sector* will overwhelm the losses in the public sector. The argument goes roughly like this: by reducing the role of government in the economy, cutting taxes, and weakening labour and environmental laws, the competitiveness and profitability of private business in Ontario will be enhanced. As a result, the province will win a larger share of export markets, and business investment will grow. Hundreds of thousands of new jobs will be created by this "outbreak of entrepreneurship."

The assumption of this approach is that somehow Ontario's jobs performance is being held back by a *lack* of profitability and competitiveness in the private business sector. A review of recent data on income distribution, the components of economic growth, and production costs in Ontario, however, questions this assumption. For example, Figure 3.11 illustrates how the growth in Ontario's economy (our nominal provincial GDP) was distributed between the different groups of our society, from 1991 up to the third quarter of 1996 (most recent data available). Total wages and salaries grew by an anemic 10% in nominal terms (which means that – after inflation – the real value of total wages and salaries hardly grew at all). Corporate profits, on the other hand, have more than doubled. Other income categories (small business and farm income, etc.) have grown barely faster than wages and salaries. With so little spending power in the hands of Ontario's consumers, is there any wonder that domestic spending in Ontario has been so sluggish? And can it really be argued that the problem holding back Ontario's economic performance is that profits are too *low*?

Figure 3.11 Ontario's Lopsided Recovery: I, Income Distribution, 1991–96

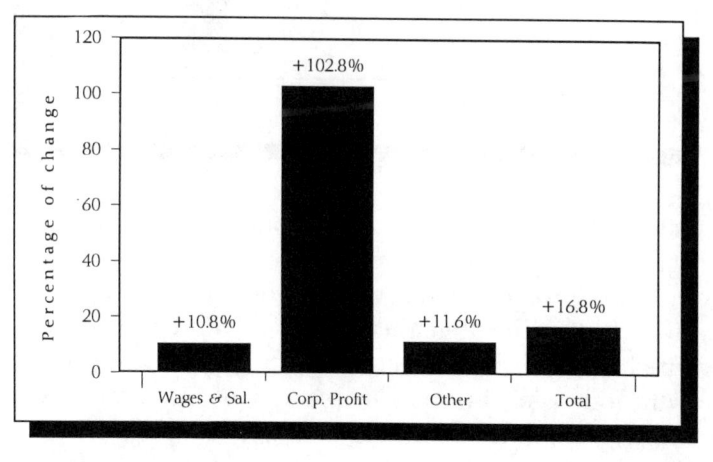

[Bar chart showing percentage of change: Wages & Sal. +10.8%, Corp. Profit +102.8%, Other +11.6%, Total +16.8%]

Similar questions are raised when the growth in Ontario's economy during the 1990s is divided according to the source of expenditure (see Figure 3.12). Overall nominal GDP in the province grew by about 17% from 1991 to the third quarter of 1996. Provincial exports grew by a staggering 64% during this time – almost four times as fast. Similarly, private business investment in machinery and equipment (the investments in factory equipment and other machinery that are considered to be particularly sensitive to an economy's competitiveness) grew by 26% – almost 60% faster than the economy as a whole. Exports and investment are the two key components of

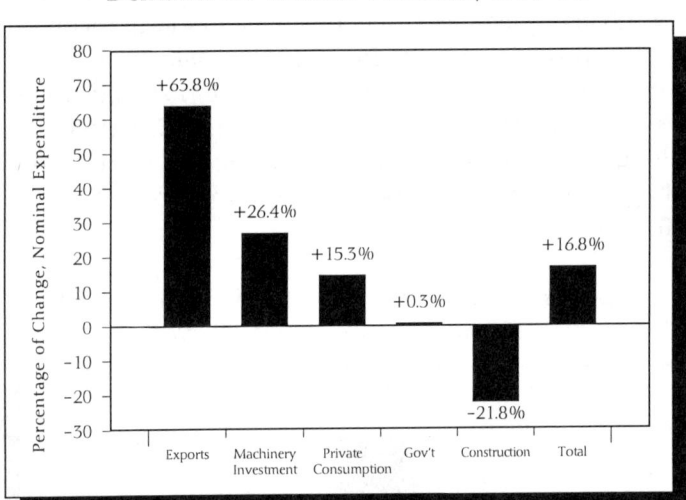

Figure 3.12 Ontario's Lopsided Recovery: II, Demand for Ontario Products, 1991–96

[Bar chart — Percentage of Change, Nominal Expenditure:
Exports +63.8%; Machinery Investment +26.4%; Private Consumption +15.3%; Gov't +0.3%; Construction −21.8%; Total +16.8%]

private-sector-led economic growth, and they have performed very impressively during the 1990s.

Ontario's problem is not that business is weak or uncompetitive, but rather that the *successes* of the export-oriented, profit-driven business sector are failing to translate into growth and rising incomes in the rest of our economy. For example, consumer spending has grown quite sluggishly during this time – more slowly than GDP as a whole has grown. This stands in contrast to the typical pattern of an economic recovery, in which booming consumer spending usually is a main engine of economic growth. Total government spending on goods and services was flat (and has declined notably since 1995). And business investment in residential and non-residential construction – spending that depends far more on the spending power of local residents than on international competitiveness or low production costs – has collapsed. Together these three sectors of the economy – private consumption, government, and construction – account for over 80% of our total GDP; despite the rhetoric in the business pages about globalization, exports, and financial investment, the growth of private households and the public sector are more important to overall economic performance. Yet these sectors have been hammered by the austerity and depression of the 1990s.

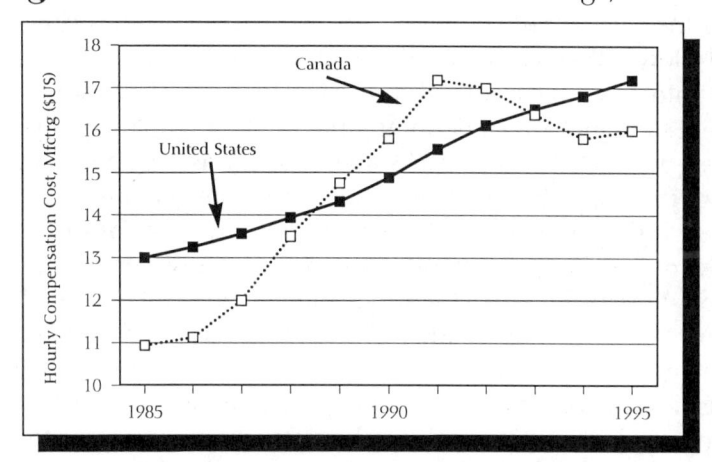

Figure 3.13 Ontario's Labour Cost Advantage, 1980–96

Can we really expect that *even faster* growth in net exports and business investment in machinery and equipment, which together account for only 20% of our economy, can possibly offset the continued stagnation of the other 80%? This would clearly require the tail to wag the economic dog. If anything, the cutbacks and deregulation agenda of the Harris government are certain to make Ontario's pattern of economic growth even *less* balanced, by undermining workers' wages and further shrinking the public sector. The very factors that have enhanced our competitiveness in the export and business sectors (low wages, unemployment, austerity) have prevented a more balanced pattern of growth from emerging. And at the same time, it is quite likely that our reliance on exports as the main engine of growth has reached its limit: export growth has already slowed markedly in the past year, and as the U.S. economy slows (as expected) over the next year or two, Ontario's economy will be extremely vulnerable if our household and public sectors are not revitalized.

Another neoconservative economic myth is that somehow Ontario's workers have "priced themselves out of world markets," and are thus responsible for their own chronic unemployment. But the most recent data shows that the total cost of labour in Ontario's all-important manufacturing sector (including the costs of employee benefits and payroll taxes) is close to 10% lower than corresponding costs in the U.S., once converted into U.S. dollars (see Figure 3.13). Can the Harris government's attempts to undermine unions, slash employer payroll costs (through WCB cutbacks and other measures), and otherwise generally cheapen the cost of labour possibly make much of a *further* improvement on Ontario's existing competitive advantage? Perhaps exports and business investment could grow marginally faster than they already are in the incredibly pro-business labour market climate that has been created in Ontario. But whatever resulting growth is experienced in the business sector will be continually undermined and offset by continued stagnation in households and our public sector – because low wages, consumer insecurity, and public sector cutbacks constitute the other side of the same Harris coin.

False Solutions Part II: Labour Market Deregulation

Another favourite argument of the Harris government and its supporters is to claim that chronic unemployment in Ontario is the result of the "over-regulation" of Ontario's labour market. They argue that government intrusions into private labour relations (through collective bargaining laws, minimum wages, pay equity, and employment standards) have made life so difficult and costly for private employers, that hiring has declined as a result. Eliminate these intrusions, allowing private employers more lee-way, and unemployment will be reduced by the "natural workings" of labour supply and demand. This thinking informs the various Harris initiatives aimed at deregulating Ontario's labour market, including: Bill 7 (which weakened collective bargaining rights); the cutbacks in social assistance and other welfare programs, and the cut in income tax rates (both of which supposedly help to restore the "incentive" to work); the curtailment or abolition of various pay equity and employment equity programs; and the proposed watering down of various employment standards (including rules governing hours of work, severance pay, and other issues).

Table 3.1 "Regulation" versus "Deregulation" in Ontario's Labour Market Outcomes

	Period of Regulation (Jan. 93 – June 95)[*]	Period of Deregulation (June 95 – April. 97)[†]
Change Employment	+164,000	+121,000
Change Unemployment	−78,000	+31,000
Change Unemployment Rate	−1.5 points	+0.3 points
Change Employment Rate	−0.4 points	−0.2 points

Notes [*] From implementation of Bill 40 to election of Harris government.

[†] From election of Harris government to present; labour market deregulation initiatives include welfare cuts, income tax cuts, Bill 7, provincial budget reductions, and announced changes to employment standards.

Source: Statistics Canada, The Labour Force (Catalogue 71-001). Seasonally adjusted data.

How valid is the initial assumption that a "free" or deregulated labour market is indeed capable of so perfectly and efficiently matching all available workers with job openings? In reality, economic history suggests that the number of people working is usually limited by the number of jobs available – not by the alleged unwillingness of unemployed people to work, nor by government interference in an otherwise well-lubricated, smoothly-functioning labour market. If it is a shortage of jobs that limits the growth of employment, will labour market deregulation produce an increase in the demand for labour (that is, in the number of jobs available)?

A disempowered, vulnerable workforce means lower wages for more work. This will benefit business (through improved profitability and competitiveness), but Ontario's corporate sector is already both profitable and competitive. Any additional improvements in investment and exports are likely to be small. At the same time, also as argued previously, consumer spending will fall (due both to lower wages and reduced government transfers to persons). This may further chill economic conditions in the consumer sector, quite likely exceeding whatever boost is given to the business sector.

Labour market deregulation is thus unlikely to create new jobs through an expansion in purchases of Ontario-made products. But the strategy might still reduce the official unemployment rate in at least two other ways – both of which are rather perverse in social terms:

- Firstly, labour force participation is likely to continue its striking and worrisome post-recession decline. Luckily for government, this trend has helped to keep the official unemployment rate under control. But by any standards the loss of the skills and energy of these discouraged workers represents a huge social and economic cost. Lowering wages and worsening working conditions can only worsen this trend.

- Secondly, the greater availability of low-wage labour, and the enhanced ability of employers to use low-wage labour in whatever profit-maximizing ways they see fit, may encourage firms to use more labour and less new capital equipment in their operations. Indeed, data already suggests that Canada's economy in recent years may already be moving in a more labour-intensive direction – which is incredibly ironic, given the pace of technological change and the need for firms to compete on grounds of technology, quality, and product innovation. (Of course, technological change itself may be contributing to the growth of low-wage, low-skill employment, as well.) Some "free-market" economists may feel that the use of low-wage labour in menial tasks as a replacement for modern capital equipment is somehow an "efficient means" of solving the unemployment crisis. But any pragmatic analysis of trends in the modern global economy would conclude that this is exactly the wrong direction for our economy to be heading in. The whole notion that an economy's potential can be enhanced by greater investment in the skills and training of its workforce is undermined when the jobs created by the economy are low-wage and low-skill. And it goes without saying that the consequences of a low-wage jobs strategy on the *quality* of work life will be severe.

On balance then, the final impact of labour-market deregulation on unemployment is uncertain at best. If weakening legal protections in the workplace (and consequently lowering wages and labour costs) has any effect in lowering unemployment, it is probably for reasons (such as lower labour force participation or the greater use of menial low-wage labour) that are neither intended nor socially beneficial. Labour-market deregulation fails to address the primary factors limiting Ontario's further economic growth: stagnant domestic spending power, an ongoing crisis of confidence among consumers, and the negative spin-off consequences of huge cutbacks in public programs.

Indeed, the evidence so far suggests that the deregulatory tendency in Ontario's labour market policies since 1995 is having, if anything, a *perverse* impact on employment and unemployment. Table 3.1 summarizes the labour market performance in Ontario under two contrasting labour market policy approaches: the more "regulationist" approach adopted by the previous NDP government (starting especially with the implementation in 1993 of the labour law reforms contained in Bill 40), and the "deregulationist" approach adopted by the subsequent government (and represented by initiatives such as the reversal of labour law reforms in Bill 7, the cuts to welfare, the elimination of pay equity and employment equity initiatives, and proposals to weaken employment standards). Did the NDP's labour market regulation kill jobs, and has the subsequent deregulation created them? In fact, the evidence summarized in Table 3.1 suggests the opposite. Job creation in Ontario has slackened considerably since the election of the Harris government. Unemployment and the unemployment rate have both increased. The aforementioned decline in the overall *employment rate* (employment as a share of the working age population) has continued.

It is unlikely that the jobs created during the lifetime of the NDP's Bill 40 had anything to do with Bill 40 itself – just as the increase in unemployment over the past year probably has had very little to do with the "free-market" shift in labour market policies. The fact is that both outcomes have been the result of broader macroeconomic trends: 1994 was a good year for Ontario's macroeconomy (the *only* good year, in fact, since the Free Trade Agreement was signed), and this (not Bill 40) accounts for the jobs that were created, while overall growth (and hence job-creation) has stagnated since then. But this is exactly the point: employment is primarily demand-constrained, dependent on spending by consumers, government, and businesses. Trying to "solve" unemployment by whittling away at what remains of workers' legal protections ignores (and may even exacerbate) the dominant economic constraints we face: low wages, pessimistic consumers, a crumbling public sector.

The Jobs Crisis and the Deficit

The dramatic and continuing deterioration in Ontario's labour market during the 1990s has contributed greatly to – indeed, has been the *dominant* cause of – the sharp escalation of Ontario's public debt burden during exactly this same time. It is hard to believe that "public overspending" created our problem, when program spending as a share of our provincial economy has been virtually unchanged (at about 15–16% of GDP) for twenty years (until now, of course, with the dramatic spending cutbacks of the Harris government). How do we explain, then, the sudden deterioration of Ontario's budget balance – from an approximate balance in

1989 to a huge deficit of some 4.5% of GDP just three years later? The simultaneous collapse in the provincial employment rate (from 67% of the working age population in 1989 to just 60% three years later) should be an obvious suspect.

Indeed, when the growth of unemployment is plotted alongside the growth of Ontario's deficit, the correlation is remarkable (as illustrated in Figure 3.14). In statistical terms, the rising unemployment rate since 1989 can "explain" 95% of the growth in the provincial deficit over the same period.[2] Viewed differently, each percentage point increase in the unemployment rate tends to increase the provincial deficit by an amount equal to 0.7% of provincial GDP (or some $2.3 billion, given current GDP levels in Ontario). In other words, the provincial government could save as much by lowering the unemployment rate by just half a point, as was saved by the 1995 cut to welfare benefit rates. Or it could finance the entire sum cut from spending by Ernie Eves' November 1995 budget by reducing the unemployment rate by a point-and-a-half.

Figure 3.14 Unemployment and the Deficit in Ontario, 1987–96

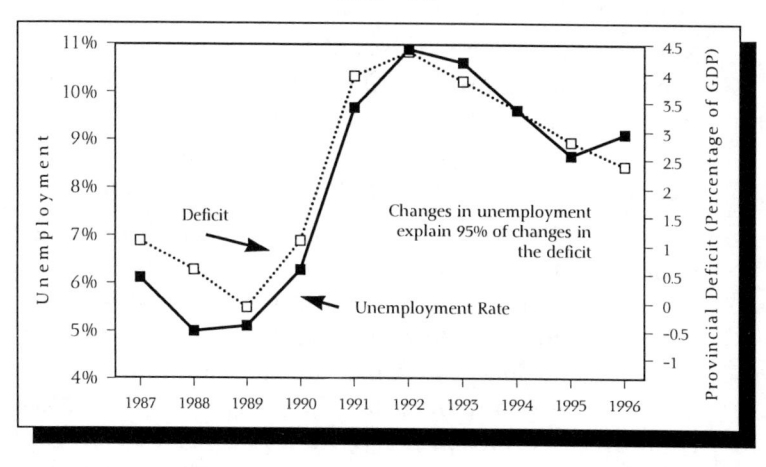

Supporters of the Harris government might argue that the causation in Figure 3.14 runs in the opposite direction –

that is, that the investor "uncertainty" and high interest rates that were allegedly caused by Ontario's large deficit undermined provincial job creation and hence created our unemployment problem. This argument is entirely unconvincing, however, for at least three major reasons:

- The chain of causation implying that "deficits cause unemployment" is indirect and uncertain. It must be shown that investors worry about public deficits in formulating their investment plans (the economic evidence on this point is virtually non-existent), and that this effect is strong enough (relative to the other factors that influence investment) to explain Ontario's slowdown and subsequent unemployment. It must also be shown that there is an equally strong and immediate link between deficits and interest rates, a point which similarly remains unproven in empirical research. In contrast, the mechanisms by which "unemployment causes deficits" are direct, immediate, and arithmetic: when people lose their jobs, they stop paying taxes, and increase their use of public assistance and income maintenance programs.

- Business investment in machinery and equipment has been one of the only *bright* spots in Ontario's economy during the 1990s. If deficits caused our unemployment, via a negative impact on "investor confidence," then this should have been one of our weakest sectors.

- *If* there is any significant negative impact of provincial deficits on real investment spending (and the evidence supporting this is meager), this must occur with a considerable time lag: allowing investors to digest news of the growing deficit, consider the impact of the deficit on their long-run business outlook, and then adjust their investment plans (which themselves are set months or even years in advance) accordingly. Similarly, if deficits caused unemployment via high interest rates, there would also be considerable time lags involved: first while financial markets digested and reacted to news of Ontario's deficit, and then one or two more years while consumers and investors reacted to the higher interest rates. But Figure 3.14 shows that employment declined step-for-step with the rise of the deficit – investors and financial markets could not even have *known* about the size of Ontario's deficit by the time that employment started falling (since current data on provincial finances takes several months to compile), let alone have already decided to increase interest rates or cut back private spending.

Figure 3.15 presents another view of the same relationship between unemployment and the provincial deficit. If the provincial unemployment rate could be reduced to 5%, the provincial budget would be rebalanced – while leaving in place every one of the public programs that existed (and were paid for!) at the time of the onset of the last recession. To reduce the unemployment rate to 5% in Ontario given our present (shrunken) labour force would require the creation of 250,000 jobs. To reduce it to 5% while allowing for the return of the discouraged workers who have left the labour market since 1990 would require the creation of at least 600,000 jobs. This would be an ambitious and radical task – but it is essential if Ontario's public finances are to be brought under control, while at the same time preserving the public programs that are crucial to the quality of life in this province. In essence, we have two choices: we can attempt to recreate the full-employment balanced budget environment of the late 1980s, creating the jobs that will allow Ontarians to pay for the services we need. Or we can follow the Harris government by attempting to slash our way to a balanced budget, while taking Ontario's depressed, underutilized, and increasingly impoverished labour market as a fact of life. For Ontarians concerned about social equality, the elimination of poverty, and the expansion of economic opportunity, the choice is clear. And for this reason, a far-reaching and highly ambitious job-creation strategy must be the centrepiece of an Alternative Budget for Ontario.

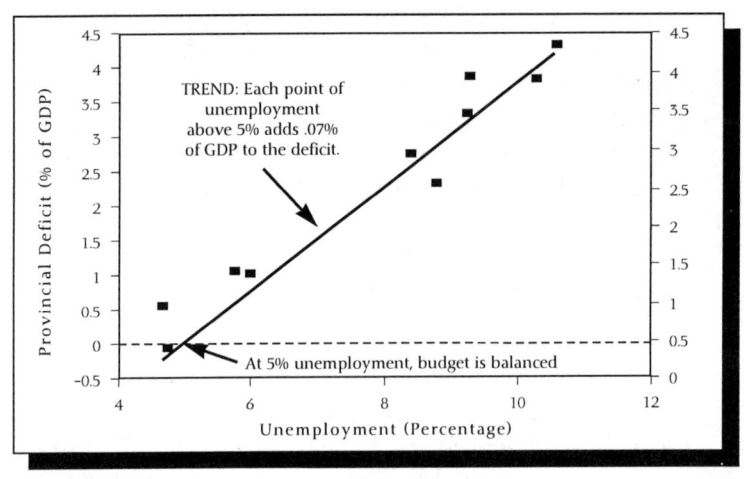

THE ONTARIO ALTERNATIVE BUDGET PAPERS

Figure 3.15 Unemployment and the Deficit in Ontario: Finding the Break-Even Point

TREND: Each point of unemployment above 5% adds .07% of GDP to the deficit.

At 5% unemployment, budget is balanced

Unemployment (Percentage)

Provincial Deficit (% of GDP)

Data Sources: The original data portrayed in Figures 3.1 through 3.7 are obtained from the Statistics-Canada's publication, *The Labour Force*. Figures 3.8 and 3.9 utilize UI beneficiary data reported in the *Canadian Economic Observer*. The data in Figure 3.10 was reported in Statistics-Canada's *Employment, Earnings and Hours*. Figures 3.11 and 3.12 utilize provincial income accounts data published by the Ontario Ministry of Finance. The data portrayed in Figure 3.13 is originally published by the U.S. Department of Labor, Bureau of Labor Statistics. Figures 3.14 and 3.15 utilize provincial finance data published by the Ontario Ministry of Finance, and unemployment data published in *The Labour Force*.

Endnotes

1 This calculation assumes that average UI benefits paid to those who qualify equal 45% of pre-layoff earnings, which reflects the experience of workers in Canada.

2 The adjusted R^2 of a regression of the provincial deficit (as a share of GDP) on the unemployment rate exceeds 0.95.

Chapter Four

WORKING DOWN OUR DEBTS: CREATING 600,000 JOBS TO REBUILD OUR COMMUNITIES

The preceeding chapter on the depth of the employment crisis in Ontario describes the precipitous decline in provincial employment that followed the recession of 1990–91. Measured as a share of our province's working age population, the provincial employment rate declined from 67% in 1989 to 60% by 1992. More worrisome, there has been *no recovery* in this employment rate since then: in fact, whatever job-creation has been experienced since the economic recovery technically began has not even been enough to keep up with the growth of our population (so that the employment rate has continued slowly to fall). The modest decline in Ontario's official unemployment rate since the end of the recession (from 11% to about 9%) has been accomplished not via job creation, but rather through the continuing decline in labour force participation. In other words, there is more bad news, not good news, lurking behind the *apparent* decline in Ontario's unemployment rate. The economic recovery of the 1990s has indeed been a grim, jobless one.

Chapter 3 also highlights the near-perfect relationship between this continuing state of crisis in Ontario's labour market and the dramatic deterioration in Ontario's provincial finances that occurred during this same time period. From an essentially balanced budget in 1989, the province's fiscal balance collapsed in step with provincial employment. The province's recent experience suggests that for each percentage point increase in provincial unemployment, the provincial deficit grows by 0.7 percentage points of GDP (or about $2.3 billion, given present levels of provicnial GDP).

To reduce the provincial unemployment rate to 5% (thus balancing the budget), while still making room for the Ontarians who have fled the labour market since the last recession, would require the immediate creation of some 600,000 jobs. In reality, of course, it will take several years to repair the damage that has been done to our labour market since 1990 – but this makes the task all the *harder*, since the economy needs to be continually generating jobs just to *keep up* with our population growth, let alone rebuild employment rates. Over the next five years, for example, if Ontario's working age population continues to grow at about 1.5% per year, Ontario will need to create over 400,000 new jobs just to maintain the employment rate at its current (depressed) level. Add to this the over 600,000 jobs needed to rebuild the employment rate back to its pre-recession peak, and the total required jobs (over five years) exceeds 1 million – or 200,000 jobs per year. Given that Ontario has created jobs at an average rate of just 75,000 per year since the bottom of the last recession, we need to more than double the pace of job creation that has been experienced so far during the current recovery.

Apart from the huge social and economic benefits that such a revitalization of the provincial labour market would generate for our households and our communities, the benefits for the province's fiscal state would be automatic and dramatic. By rebuilding Ontario's employment rate to its pre-recession peak – in short, by finding jobs for the 7 in 100 working age Ontarians who *used* to work and pay taxes, but now no longer do so – we could repair the fiscal basis for the public programs and services that made such a contribution to our province's economic and social development in previous decades. In short, we could *both* preserve (and even expand) provincial programs, while simultaneously balancing the province's books and ultimately reducing our debt burden.

So the fundamental starting point of the Job-Creation Committee of the Ontario Alternative Budget Project has been our recognition of the need to repair the huge damage done to our job market during the 1990s. This will require some far-reaching, visionary, even radical measures. The retrenchment of private-sector employment and investment in our post-free-trade, zero-inflation macroeconomic regime has been severe, and has been exacerbated by the unprecedented rollback of public-sector employment and services-provision at all levels of government. Moreover, there is no indication that the supposed restoration of Ontario's (and Canada's) so-called economic "fundamentals" – such as our low inflation, disappearing budget deficits, shrinking public sector, and deregulated, competitive private sector – will in any way fundamentally improve the long-term jobs outlook. In short, "what you see is what you get": without an urgent change in policy direction, chronic unemployment in the 8–10% range, together with stagnant wages and growing inequality, will be the norm.

We recognize also the tremendous constraints that have been placed on Ontario's labour market by macroeconomic policies implemented at the federal level, and by other national or international economic developments that are largely beyond the control of any provincial government. The jobs crisis of the 1990s in Ontario was the clear result of free-trade and high-interest-rate policies pursued by the federal government; our subsequent stagnation has been greatly aided by huge cutbacks in federal program spending. The reversal of these destructive policies would go a long ways toward solving Ontario's economic woes (as demonstrated, for example, in the Alternative Federal Budget). Nevertheless, we limit our attention here to policies that could be pursued provincially – while admitting that the broader macroeconomic context has made our effort to recreate full-employment in Ontario dramatically harder.

To turn around our present depressing scenario will require urgent action indeed. But without a full-employment strategy for Ontario, the balancing of the province's books will be incredibly expensive (in terms of reduced program spending). So our committee has set itself the goal of visioning how 600,000 extra jobs could be created and filled in Ontario (*on top of* the new jobs required just to keep up with population growth), as the foundation for a progressive solution to our province's debt and deficit woes. A considerable amount of progress will be made on the jobs front merely by reversing the dramatic cutbacks in public programs that have been implemented over the past two years: these have directly eliminated tens of thousands of jobs in the broader public service, and thousands more that have been destroyed by the negative macroeconomic spin-off effects of government cutbacks. So perhaps 150,000 jobs would be directly created in the provincial economy by the rebuilding of core public programs that is described in the other chapters of this document. But even this achievement, while impressive, puts us only one-quarter of the way towards repairing the damage that has been done to Ontario's job market during the jobless 1990s.

What is presented here, therefore, is not a final program for job-creation. Instead, we offer some initial thoughts about two prominent components of a wider-ranging progressive jobs strategy: the creation of locally-based "full-employment councils" to address local unemployment, and the reduction of average hours of work. This agenda will be developed and expanded through the consultations and discussions that will occur over the next year as part of the Ontario Alternative Budget process.

Put People to Work Addressing Community Needs: Community Full-Employment Councils

Local Labour Market Planning in the Next Century

The objective of the Ontario Alternate Budget is to increase employment and create a more egalitarian and democratic Ontario, in a fiscally-responsible manner. This is a long-term objective, that will ultimately involve substantially transforming our reliance on private market forces, and expanding forms of democratic governance – including democratic governance over our economy. For employment policy, this long-run goal centres on the issues of increasing the quantity of jobs and redistributing hours of work more equally, to eliminate unemployment. But we also aim to improve the *quality of work* through training and higher labour standards; to *re-direct labour* into those sectors which are expanding thanks to growing market demand; and to expand employment in *non-market sectors* that are producing socially-necessary goods or providing more egalitarian access to services.

In the short and medium term, these goals can be promoted by reorienting some of the province's budgetary goals, as outlined in the other chapters of this document. But it will also require, in the long run, developing and expanding non-market institutions that will increase our democratic capacity to plan employment and to intervene in local labour markets. Not all of the people all of the time can exercise direct control over the social and economic changes which affect their employment and communities. But we can ensure that citizens are more fully informed about the economic processes which affect their employment opportunities, and we can establish political structures which will allow for greater citizens' participation aimed at enhancing people's capacities to contribute to democratic, strategic economic interventions around employment. To do this we need to re-establish a credible employment planning process – both at the federal and provincial levels, but also at the community level, in order to actively intervene in job creation and local labour markets. We need to develop a different kind of employment planning process which will empower communities, workers, and unions to actively participate in controlling, shaping and determining the future of work in our community. This can be summarized as developing institutions and capacities that work "in and against the market."

We believe that local employment planning will be central to creating and sustaining full employment. The long-term changes to employment that have occurred over this century in Ontario imply that most employment and job growth will occur in urban communities, where the vast majority of our population live and work. But even in rural areas, employment growth is concentrated in activities in local communities, rather than being dispersed across the agricultural sector or resource activities. Indeed, employment in these latter two sectors – agriculture and resources – is well under 10% of total employment, and will continue to fall. So the vast majority of employment is in manufacturing (which we would hope to hold stable at a constant share of total employment) and more importantly in services. The idea of community full-employment councils recognizes that the future of work is concentrated in *local communities*. It recognizes that local economic conditions are increasingly important – in an era when national and even provincial boundaries are less important in economic terms – to the creation and maintenance of good jobs. Finally, it also recognizes that improving and expanding the quality of services (public and private) will be central to the future of work in Ontario.

There is a desperate need to formulate local labour plans which account for the existing labour stock and skills, and that forecast local labour force trends, skill shortages, and employment trends. This kind of detailed knowledge cannot be found or developed at the federal or even provincial level – beyond simply summarizing broad trends. To tackle the unemployment crisis, local labour market authorities – our community full-employment councils – must become more forward-looking and active, rather than acting solely as passive dispensers of income support payments or centres for the video display of job postings.

There is an added dimension to developing local employment councils and planning capacities that we want to stress as part of the vision and strategy underlying the Ontario Alternative Budget. In the service sector, where most job growth will occur, the challenge is not to only raise the quality of work and pay, but also to collectivize many service activities that are unavailable to many because of income restraints (as with daycare), or are not available at all because of underfunding. This will require budgetary and tax policies at the provincial level to collect and redistribute resources across the province. But it is equally impossible to envision this being done without planning of resource use and input from the local users and producers of the services. It is not possible to provide adequate library resources in a multi-cultural society, for example, from an office tower at Queen's Park. Decentralized popular planning should be central to a non-market "third sector" – that is, self-managed community services such as cultural production, environmental clean-up, education and leisure. These activities will have to be planned, through local labour market boards, to determine socially-useful activities, community needs, and local skills. This reinforces the linkages between the expansion of employment and the formation of the democratic capacity to manage our economy that lies behind our conception of community full-employment councils.

A complementary goal of our emphasis on local employment planning is to extend the role of democratic administration in our economy. Postwar Keynesianism concentrated on centralized aggregate demand management, with little economic planning. It was recognized that employment planning and adjustment policies were a necessary supplement to demand management in tight labour markets. But this remained limited to forecasting broader occupational and labour force trends. The local component of planning, in turn, was limited to "labour exchanges" which served largely as locations for job listings and counselling. They never did much in the way of identifying local job or skill needs. In Canada, even these limited services provided by Employment Centres have been undermined by federal cutbacks over the past decade. By the mid-1990s, Canada had virtually no national labour market strategy or local intelligence centres. Canada and Ontario now have the worst of all possible worlds for labour market policy: mass unemployment, but no central or local labour market and employment planning capacities to attempt to deal with that unemployment.

How might community full-employment councils operate? They would be composed of directly-elected representatives from each community (with representation potentially supplemented by members of community organizations). The objective of each council would be to promote and facilitate communities' definition of their own economic and employment needs, and develop popular strategies for economic (as well as cultural and political) projects that can meet those needs. The councils would work closely with local city government, local economic planning bureaus, local business, and community organizations to develop an inventory of community needs. Each council would sponsor popular meetings to encourage debate and deliberation over these community needs, consider large-scale projects falling within the community, and work out in detail through community involvement a future vision for the community. The councils would not simply create another level of government, but would enhance the efficiency of planning and development in the community in general, by providing a formal means of generating community input that will avoid the problems that plagued past ad hoc approaches.

Careful foresight, sensitive leadership and the mobilization of progressive opinion can ensure that this devolution of labour market planning power to the local level does not lead to the "offloading" of difficult social problems onto other communities and thus to the exacerbation of inequalities. The legal mandate of the full-employment councils would forbid the offloading of problems onto neighbouring jurisdictions; province-wide standards would need to be observed; and local developments could not violate provincial employment plans and standards. Funding for local initiatives would be conditional on the assumption of responsibilities for social solidarity, with the distribution of funds deliberately oriented toward those poorer communities that have the greatest social needs.

The councils would have real powers, including a mandate to conduct hearings in their locale over development projects beyond a certain size. But these powers would go beyond the negative right of local veto to the positive right – and the necessary resources – to initiate, qualify, amend, or further specify employment plans as they apply to their areas. In this regard, the full-employment councils would be distinguished from past initiatives aimed at facilitating labour adjustment or local and sectoral planning (such as the previous OTAB initiatives in Ontario), which were granted broad mandates but few resources and virtually no decision-making powers.

More ambitiously the full-employment councils could expand their social and economic responsibilities such that they play a role analogous to Boards of Education. Just as the latter fulfil their statutory mandate of providing places in the school system for each child and youth in their catchment area (to a considerable extent through funding provided by higher levels of government), so must the community full-employment councils, with their mandate of securing employment or training for every willing adult in their community, be so funded. The councils' role would be to initiate or respond to projects that fulfil this mandate; to develop particular local priorities such as improved training and skills development, better transportation, co-op housing, community centres, child care and care for the aged; and to generally participate in a radical reworking of our ideas about employment and training.

The establishment of community full-employment councils would constitute a radical departure in the structure both of city government (recognizing the increasing importance of the local economic entity), and of labour market planning. The potential of this approach is dramatic. Full-employment councils open up the possibility of renewed prosperity – a prosperity which is congruent with the values of equity and community, and not just with the dictates of the market. While this is an ambitious plan, the powers and responsibilities of the councils could be expanded gradually over several years. It would be important to establish the councils sooner rather than later, however, so as to lay a foundation for the development of local democratic planning skills.

Three Tasks of the Community Full-Employment Councils

We propose the establishment of democratically-controlled full-employment councils in each local economic jurisdiction. Their general mandate would be to intervene in the functioning of the local labour market (on both the supply and the demand sides of that market), so as to ensure that all willing and able workers in the local economy have the opportunity to become gainfully employed in decently-paying jobs. The specific functions of these councils would be three-fold:

1) Labour Market Planning

The local full-employment councils would consolidate and coordinate existing labour force training, adjustment, and restructuring programs that are already offered by various levels of government. Part of the councils' mandate would be to conduct inventories of local labour resources, as well as unmet local infrastructure or community needs. This will facilitate a better "matching" of unemployed or displaced workers with jobs as they become available. The funding for this function of the local councils could be amalgamated from funding that is presently directed to various training and adjustment programs, and perhaps from targetted social assistance savings (gained by finding real jobs for workers currently receiving social assistance). Targetted funding for training programs could be obtained from a refundable training tax on local employers (paid back to those employers who meet a target level of in-house training expenditure for their existing employees).

2) Local Industrial Policy

The local full-employment councils would work to identify the local economic resources (labour, knowledge, technology, space, and natural resources) that could be marshalled in the development of important new local industries (including service-providing industries). It would help to identify emerging industrial opportunities, and then put the identified resources "into action" – that is, playing the economic role of the "entrepreneur," in sectors in which private entrepreneurs are not doing a sufficiently expansive job of it. This locally-developed industrial strategy would reflect the principles of *community economic development*, but writ large: communities collectively identifying the resources they have available to develop new economic opportunities for their populace.

Capital supplied by a provincial Public Investment Bank, and then allocated to the local full-employment councils to fund locally-based projects, would play a central role in financing and facilitating new projects; additional private funds could be leveraged on the basis of this initial, publicly-supplied seed money. Initial funding for the Public Investment Bank would be provided through taxes on Ontario banks and other financial insitutions, as well as through the compulsory deposit of a very small share of the assets of provincially-regulated pension funds. This recognizes the failure of our private financial system to independently inject enough capital resources needed to employ our idle citizens. It would also help to address, to some extent, the huge and unacceptable gap between the historic profits being generated in Ontario's financial industry on the one hand, and the stagnation and pessimism sadly typical of our *real* economy on the other.

3) Social and Public Services Delivery

Perhaps the most ambitious (and expensive) task of the local full-employment councils would be to directly generate employment opportunities in the provision of services and tasks aimed at improving the quality of life in local communities. The basic quandary presently facing Ontarians is as follows. On the one hand, Ontario is experiencing a tremendous need for investment in our economic, social, environmental, and cultural infrastructure: there are literally hundreds of needs crying out for attention, and local communities can identify these needs better than anyone. On the other hand, we have idle resources (especially labour) which could be set into motion in the fulfillment of these needs – were it not for the budget constraints imposed by the chronic lack of effective demand which characterizes our private-sector economy. The full-employment councils will be the vehicle that matches unmet needs with unemployed resources. Much as the U.S. Works Progress Administration attempted, during the 1930s, to provide emergency funding to allow unemployed labour to address concrete community needs, the full-employment councils will be given resources to play the same role, in the context of our labour market emergency of the 1990s.

We would like to allocate an amount equivalent to the cost of the Harris income tax cut (approximately $5 billion per year, once fully implemented) to the direct provision of social and community services by the local councils. In this way we are demonstrating that the true way to create jobs in Ontario is not to cut services and pump the savings back into (disproportionately well-off) private households, but instead to fund community efforts to come together to collectively meet their own social and economic needs.

Together with monies potentially available from other sources (such as federal infrastructure program funds), this level of funding would allow for the creation and support of as many as 120,000 jobs in the direct provision of these services (at an average total cost of some $50,000 per job). Perhaps ways could be found to provide a share of the compensation offered to participating workers in the form of goods and services that are actually produced by the public works program itself; for example, if a community public works initiative places a priority on building non-profit local housing, then some of the compensation offered to participating workers could take the form of subsidized or free occupancy of that non-profit housing. In this case, the initial level of cash funding could create even more jobs.

The funds would be allocated to facilitate projects in four key program areas: our traditional "concrete" infrastructure (roads, sewers, other local infrastructure), our "social" infrastructure (community and public programs), environmental conservation and reconstruction, and culture. Employment priority will be given to target groups who have been particularly hard-hit by the ongoing jobs crisis of the 1990s: youth, other target groups (workers of colour, women, the disabled), and social assistance recipients. In the latter case, the public provision of *real* jobs, at decent rates of pay, with full labour rights, performing concrete, valuable tasks in local communities, would constitute our progressive alternative to the workfare program of the Harris government.

The idea of locally-based full employment planning is novel and far-reaching, and obviously the sketch provided above leaves numerous issues undefined, and numerous questions unanswered. Our hope is that the process of grass-roots consultation and participation which will be initiated by the Ontario Alternative Budget project over the next year will address some of these outstanding issues:

- How would the full-employment councils be elected/chosen? How would the democratic accountability of these councils be ensured? How could their work be linked with other local planning tasks (such as education, economic development, infrastructure and environmental planning, etc.)? How would the creation of these councils relate to the process of restructuring municipal government?

- How would the jurisdictions for which the full-employment councils function be determined? Yes, job-creation is increasingly "local" – but how local is "local"? Should councils be established in smaller towns, or at the level of regional municipalities? Would there be a full-employment council for the GTA? For Metro Toronto? For each community within the GTA?
- How could we ensure that the full-employment councils do not become a "bureaucratic" entity that is as far-removed from the community as are existing government bodies?
- How could the work of the local councils be coordinated on the provincial or regional level, to ensure that labour market issues that are not purely "local" in nature can be effectively addressed?
- What role would/should private businesses play in the work of the full-employment councils? Will business want to participate? What (if any) incentives should be offered to encourage this participation? How much power/veto-right should the business sector be given?
- Would the full-employment councils have sufficient funds to support the necessary level of local job-creation? What other sources of funding could be tapped? Are there ways in which the councils could generate their *own* sources of funding (through, for example, the partial "sale" of council-provided services such as housing or child care)?
- How would we ensure that fair employment practices are respected in the jobs that are created/funded by the full-employment councils? How would we ensure that the projects of the councils do not undermine existing employment elsewhere in the public sector?

Redistributing Work and Leisure: Reducing Working Hours in the Long-Term

Shorter working time has long been a favourite policy proposal of social activist and labour organizations. Indeed, the prospect of redistributing the existing demand for labour more widely across the working age population would seem to hold great potential both for reducing unemployment and for improving the quality of life for the presently employed. For example, suppose that the average annual working hours of Ontario's current 4.3 million full-time employed persons could be reduced (over some years) by about 4% (equivalent, roughly, to an additional two weeks off work each year, or a reduction in weekly hours of work from 40 to 38.5), in a manner that required the hiring of replacement workers to cover the lost time. The end result could be the creation of some 175,000 new full-time positions.

Ironically, the Harris government is moving in the opposite direction – proposing to *weaken* legislation governing working hours and overtime, so as to give employers a freer hand in organizing work and cutting costs. Canada (and Ontario) already rank very poorly, by OECD standards, in terms of our long annual working hours. The social consequences of promoting *longer* working hours, and thus widening the gap between Ontario and most of the rest of the industrialized world, will be visible in higher levels of stress, more workplace health and safety problems, and less healthy families. We fall firmly in the opposing camp: we want to achieve shorter working hours, both so that existing work can be distributed more fairly within society, and so that workers can have a better quality of life while on and off the job.

However, there are numerous potential pitfalls and controversies encountered in determining more specifically how working hours are to be reduced, if the final outcome (reducing average lifetime working hours) is to be achieved in a fair and employment–enhancing manner. Initial discussions of this issue by the Job–Creation Committee agreed upon a number of common principles that should guide our working time policy proposals; we then list a menu of potential policy tools that could be considered in the course of attempting to implement shorter working time. Once again, discussion of this broad policy option by progressives in Ontario over the next year will be crucial in shaping our final, more specific proposals. We wish to acknowledge the important input we have already received from the 32 Hours for Full Employment committee.

Principles: Reducing Working Time in a Progressive Way

A central reason for the recent tendency for many Ontarians to work *longer* hours has been the incredible economic insecurity faced by working people in the jobless 1990s. One response to that economic insecurity – the difficulty of finding work, the high risk of losing it, stagnant or declining wages – has been for employees to work extra hours when they *are* employed, thus attempting to provide some financial cushion against future job loss or declining real incomes. In order to reduce working hours in a progressive, participatory way, therefore, this chronic insecurity must be resolved. If Ontarians could be confident that they could find decent work when they wanted or needed it, then they would be all the more willing to work *less hours* (by working shorter hours each week, taking time off for family or education, or retiring early) when they wanted or needed extra time. Our efforts to rebuild a full-employment economic environment in Ontario, and improve the labour standards which govern the conditions of work and the terms of employment, will serve as important building blocks in the simultaneous effort to win support for shorter working time.

Within the current context of insecurity and inequality, however, it is also important that shorter working time initiatives be designed so that workers are affected in a fair manner by whatever new rules or incentives are put in place. For this reason, the following basic principles should be respected in the ultimate design of any shorter working time package:

- Our general goal is to reduce the lifetime annual average hours of work per employee, within a context of full-employment and economic security.
- The reduction in working time cannot be a policy of "shared austerity," by which a group of already underemployed and insecure individuals simply share their poverty more equally. We do not accept unemployment, macroeconomic stagnation, and growing inequality as the parameters within which working time issues must be considered. The working hours and incomes of low-paid and part-time workers must be protected as a first priority in any shorter working time strategy.
- Shorter work-time initiatives must also be applied to professional and salaried workers. It cannot simply be blue-collar or hourly workers who are subject to new regulations (simply because it is easier to "measure" or "control" their working hours). Salaried workers are among those most victimized by the lack of enforcement of current working time regulations, and hence they also have much to gain from working-time reduction policies.
- We view shorter working time as an important economic strategy in light of the environmental constraints limiting extensive economic growth. Enjoying the benefits of higher productivity in the form of more leisure time, rather than more consumption of material goods, is quite consistent with the need to develop an environmentally sustainable pattern of economic growth and job-creation.

An Agenda of Policy Options

The various specific means by which government policy could promote the reduction of average working hours can be grouped into the following three categories:

1) Legislative Reductions of Working Hours:
   - reduce the standard work week (at present in Ontario it is 44 hours)
   - require overtime to be paid, and give workers the right to refuse overtime, after a shorter number of hours per week or per day (at present in Ontario workers can refuse overtime after 48 hours work in a week, and the government wants to increase this to 50; employers must pay overtime premiums after 40 hours in a week, with no daily limit)
   - limit the number of hours of overtime per year for which compensation can be paid, rather than offered in compensating time off (The Donner commission recommended 100 hours maximum paid overtime per year)
   - better minimum standards for annual vacations (at present employers are only required to offer 2 weeks paid vacation after one year service); compulsory vacations (prohibiting the payment of paid compensation in lieu of vacation time-off)
   - improve the rights of employees to unpaid or subsidized personal, family and educational leaves

2) Better Enforcement of Existing Working Hours Legislation:
   - existing employment standards regarding hours of work, vacations, etc., could be better enforced by government
   - employees could be made better aware of their legal rights (and thus more able to independently demand these rights from their employers) through educational efforts by government
   - employment standards regarding maximum hours of work, overtime pay, etc., are especially badly enforced for salaried workers

3) Creating Incentives for Voluntary Reductions of Working Time:
- some voluntary reductions in working hours can be accomplished through collective bargaining agreements, while others are reflected in individual or personal terms of employment
- reduce the relative importance of fixed employment benefit costs (which make overtime relatively more attractive for employers) by socializing costs such as supplementary health, drug, and dental benefits
- convert other fixed employment costs to variable employment costs, by removing the ceiling on payroll taxes (such as EI or CPP premiums)
- discourage overtime and long hours of work by increasing the minimum overtime premium that must be paid to workers, collecting extra payroll taxes on overtime hours, or collecting a special tax on overtime
- offer tax subsidies to firms that reduce average working hours and hence expand their employment
- offer protection for individual employees wishing to reduce their working hours, from threats of dismissal, non-promotion, etc. (that is, guarantee employees the "Right to Work Less")
- improve the conditions faced by part-time workers (including requiring the provision of non-wage employment benefits on a pro-rated basis) so that more workers will individually choose reduced working hours

On the subject of shorter working time, too, there are many unanswered questions and unresolved controversies. These are some of the issues that need to be considered in the coming province-wide consultations.

- How many jobs, realistically, can be created by reducing working hours?

- Should legislation be used to reduce working time, or should the focus be placed instead on promoting voluntary measures?

- How can proposals for shorter working time simultaneously make room for the need of many low-wage, part-time, or contingent workers for *more* working time?

- To what extent is the reduction of working hours predicated on continuing productivity growth (so that material living standards do not decline with working time)? How can shorter working time be promoted in an era of slower or non-existent productivity growth?

Part III

Rebuilding Services

Chapter Five

EDUCATION: TOWARDS TOMORROW

Introduction

The current Minister of Education and Training has often argued that the current allocation for the elementary and secondary education in Ontario is quite sufficient and that significant savings – while improving the quality of the "product" – could be achieved by restructuring the way in which education funds are expended. Others have pointed to a crisis in equity – certain school boards have greater access to locally controlled funds than others and that what is required is a re-allocation of existing funds between boards.

This paper is written from a different premise. The school funding problem that Ontario faces is not – as the Minister would say – the more efficient use of a diminishing fund. Nor is it the need to more equitably allocate the present amount. The real crisis is that Ontario is simply not spending enough on the education of its children. The crisis is one of *adequacy* not efficiency or equity.

The writer of this paper was asked to deal with the following issue: *What is a sufficient level of expenditure?* This question leads to others. Who is to be educated? What should be taught? How? Should the education experience be inclusive? Should the curriculum be rich, diverse and challenging or should publicly funded education merely strive to provide the basic literacies needed to survive in today's world? Should our schools attempt to help students overcome disadvantage and disability? Is publicly funded education a cost or an investment? In short, the question of *how much* a community should spend on education must be dealt with within a broader paradigm of the role of education in our society.

What envelope of services and opportunities should be available in our schools? The following list is appropriate for an egalitarian, democratic society.

- Educational opportunity should be available to all, equitably, without regard to personal circumstance, place of residence, heritage, race or religion.

- Schools must be provided with the physical resources required for learning – safe, clean comfortable facilities, texts and other learning materials.

- Students must have good access to dedicated, empowered teachers and other education workers.

- The curriculum should be rich and varied, providing all students with the literacies required in today's society and each student with the opportunity to excel.

- Elementary and secondary education should be the start of a lifetime of learning.

- Elementary and secondary education should be available to all without impediment and thus should be free of any and all fees payable by students and/or their parents and should be provided in schools sustained exclusively by public funds.

- Publicly funded elementary and secondary education is the primary mechanism by which a democratic society passes its values on to the next generation.

- School boards and school councils should have the autonomy to manage schools in the interest of their communities within provincially set frameworks and have the independent access to resources sufficient to that task.

As this paper was being prepared, the Ontario government introduced *Bill 104: The Fewer School Boards Act, 1997*. In addition the Minister of Education announced a set of school finance proposals which, if carried out, would take the power to tax from school boards and, as a result, remove the fiscal autonomy presently enjoyed by boards of trustees. The premises behind *Bill 104* are incompatible with those of this paper.

Establishing an Adequate Level Of Funding

Money Does Matter

A common theme found within neo-conservative attacks on public school expenditure is that there is no correlation between the amount of money spent and student achievement. By extension this would mean that having smaller classes, experienced and well-prepared and adequately supported teachers, plentiful and up-to-date learning resources, opportunities for learning experiences, safe and comfortable classrooms, etc. do not affect student learning.

There is a growing body of evidence that, when public school systems chose additional expenditures over "restructuring," students benefit. Most of the relevant studies are American. Selected American studies suggest the following:

- **A richer, more varied curriculum flows from higher spending levels**. Evidence given in a paper presented by Harper Dean of the University of Maine at the 1996 Conference of the American Education Finance Association (AEFA), showed that the higher spending schools in Maine had substantially more vocational, math, science, social studies, foreign language and advanced placement courses than the lower spending ones.

- **Additional expenditure leads to more for the classroom**. In a paper presented to the 1995 Conference of the AEFA Yasser A. Nakib of USCLA presented evidence which suggested that higher spending Florida school districts allocated a greater percentage of their (larger) expenditures to instruction.

- **Additional expenditure leads to smaller classes.** In a paper presented to the 1995 AEFA Conference, Monk and Roelke presented evidence that suggested that teachers saw fewer pupils in high-spending school districts in New York State than teachers in low-spending districts.

- **Input inequities are strongly linked to outcome inequalities.** Robert Berne in *Outcome Equity in Education* observes that, when comparing New York State schools, there is a strong and consistent relationship between outcomes such as test sources and variables such as school district type, poverty status and minority composition. Thus for New York and other large urban districts, for high-poverty and high-minority schools, outcomes are substantially poorer. Berne argues that additional equalizing resources are necessary in such cases to offset the additional obstacles to student achievement.

- **More money succeeds where reorganization fails.** In a paper presented to the 1993 AEFA Conference two large, urban-core, mid-western cities were compared. At the start of the longitudinal study Chicago and St. Louis had comparable problems – poverty, large minority presence, significant unemployment and troubled schools. If anything the students in St. Louis faced greater deprivation. In 1980 the school systems spent approximately the same amounts per pupil, $2,640 in St. Louis and $2,720 in Chicago. Over the next twelve years, St. Louis pulled ahead of Chicago in expenditure. In 1992 St. Louis spent $7,793 per pupil and Chicago spent $5,868. In Chicago the attempt to improve schools took the form of reform of school governance – powers were devolved to what were essentially school councils – without increased revenues. In comparing the changes within the two school systems, the authors found that in St. Louis, the school district was able to bolster its regular education program while providing additional student support and upgrading a deteriorating physical plant. Chicago, on the other hand, had to cut staff and struggled to keep up with inflationary cost increases.

The payoff for St. Louis for its additional expenditures has been improved retention rates and higher test scores (one would expect increased retention to depress scores). Chicago, over the same period, has experienced increasing dropout rates and stagnant test scores.

- **An investment in early childhood education pays off.** *Approaching Kindergarden*, a report released by an agency of the U.S. Department of Education, the National Center for Education Statistics (NCES), shows that attending Head Start, prekindergarten or other centre-based preschool programs is linked to higher emerging literacy scores in 4-year-olds. The increase attributable to such programs is statistically significant even when other child and family characteristics are controlled. The report also found that this benefit of preschool attendance accrues to children from both high-risk and low-risk family backgrounds.

- **In the United States as a whole, rising academic achievements are occurring simultaneously with increasing average expenditure.** The NCES reports that – in constant value 1994–5 dollars – per pupil expenditure rose from an average US$4,909 in 1983–4 to US$6,857 in 1994–5 (CAN$6,136 to CAN$8,571). During that same period measures were taken to encourage students to increase the academic content of their high school experience – particularly in mathematics and science. There has been a significant improvement. The American experience strongly suggests that education curriculum reforms can be successful if accompanied by additional revenues.

The American experience reveals that improving our schools is inextricably linked to improving funding for our schools.

Some General Principles of Education Finance

1) **Funding should be adequate to the intended purpose.** In the past Ontario has established arbitrary per pupil expenditure ceilings – expenditure amounts that appear to have been based on the funds the government was prepared to make available rather than on the cost of the required service. At the same time, the government has required school boards to take on additional programs without giving recognition to additional cost. The funding model *must* reflect a realistic assessment of the resources needed for the required tasks.

2) **Funding should be equitable.** Equitable for whom? There are three categories of recipients of equitable treatment – the students, the boards of trustees and the ratepayers.

    Equity for Students means access to the required resources without impediment due to personal circumstance, geographic location or local ability to raise taxes. To achieve student equity it is generally recognized that there must be (i) equal treatment of equal requirements and (ii) unequal treatment where the requirements are unequal. For example, students should have access to the same resources despite variations in local taxing wealth (an illustration of the first type of student equity) and should have access to additional resources where costs are higher or when *additional* services are required.

    Equity for Boards of Trustees means that school boards would have equal access to the same level of autonomous (i.e. trustee-controlled) revenues despite local taxing wealth for a given level of taxing effort.

    Equity for Ratepayers means that the local tax burden, for equal levels of service, must be equal.

3) **The funding model should provide for a balance of authority and responsibility between the provincial government and local authorities.** Elementary and secondary education began in Ontario as a local enterprise. The independence of boards of trustees from municipal councils was, from the beginning, understood to be necessary to ensure that the education of young people did not take a back seat to other municipal priorities. Over the years, provincial and even national educational issues have come to the fore. These issues include: establishing a uniform, adequate curriculum, ensuring that adequate standards of educational service delivery are established and maintained, ensuring that schools are funded adequately and equitably, ensuring that all residents have the set of necessary skills and abilities to take their place in the community and the nurturing of the human capital of the province. On the other hand, (i) schools still work best when the decision makers are close at hand, and (ii) the school is often the most important resource in the community; and the community, especially the parents, has a strong sense of "ownership" and wish to have some control over what goes on in it.

What is needed then is both a balance of fiscal control and authority between the provincial and local authorities. At present, Ontario has the worst of both worlds. Successive governments have off-loaded most of the fiscal burden to the local rate-payers, thereby endangering both adequate and equitable funding. And now the current government plans to seize fiscal control through its funding reform proposals and its school governance changes. In 1975 Ontario government grants (GLGs) funded 61.31% of all school board costs, with local revenues making up the rest. In the 1996–7 year GLGs may support as little as 32% of school board costs. A return to the 60% funding level – with a funding model designed to provide adequacy, coupled with unfettered school board access to local revenues, would help re-establish that balance of authority between local and provincial decision makers.

4) **Public funds for elementary and secondary education should go solely to publicly-funded school boards.** Charter school funding or voucher funding or per capita payments to private schools undermine both community control over its schools and adequate, equitable funding for students. None of these funding arrangements should be supported in any way.

What goods and services are required to educate students?

1) **Students require schools with safe, comfortable, appropriate facilities.** Such facilities would include classrooms, libraries, cafeterias, labs, gyms, shops and various instructional support facilities such as caretakers' quarters, school offices, preparation rooms and storage areas. Once erected, schools need to be well maintained, kept in good repair and renovated to meet emerging health and safety standards and changing circumstances.

The present Minister of Education and others have expressed the view that the services required to maintain and repair schools could be provided more efficiently if an outside agency or contractor provided those services to school boards. The supposed benefits are illusory – contracting out leads to higher costs and reduced services. One special concern, the adults in a school – no matter what the role – are part of a team that nurtures and supports students and provides them with an environment in which they can learn and grow. In addition, although it may not be part of the nominal job description, the contact that clerical, caretaking and other support staff have with individual students can have profound effect. The contracting out of clerical or plant operations functions has the potential to impair the efficient delivery of service and, indeed, may endanger students.

2) **Students require good access to qualified, well prepared teachers and educational support staff.** This means classroom teachers, special education teach-

ers, teacher–librarians, guidance teachers, principals, secretaries, caretakers, technicians of all sorts, social workers, psychologists and psychometrist. Because of individual circumstance, some students will require additional staff to provide equal access to educational opportunity.

The smaller staffs in Ontario schools – due to continuous staff reductions over the last five years – mean larger classes and narrowed curricula, as well as reduced access to those services such as counselling, remedial services, special education and ESL which equalize the access to educational opportunity.

3) **Students require good access to learning materials and learning experiences.** Students need up-to-date texts, well-stocked libraries, properly-equipped science labs, computers and other hardware, up-to-date software appropriate to the implementation of computer technologies across the curriculum. As technological developments in our society race ahead, technological teachers need to be re-trained and shops re-vamped to provide the new technological fundamentals to students. Our students also need to be able to go out of the schools, electronically and personally to learn those things that cannot be taught in the classroom.

4) **For many students, particularly in rural areas, access to education means taking a bus to school.** Although efficiencies can be obtained by adopting new transportation patterns such as employing a single transportation system for all students moving within a single region, school bus expenditures can not be eliminated or significantly reduced without affecting access to education.

5) **Efficient administration provides the climate in which students can learn.** Some oversight is required to ensure that the educational goods and services which students require are provided for in an efficient fashion. In 1995 administrative costs beyond the school level – except for instructional supervision – consumed 3.1% of elemen-

tary panel costs and 3.7% of secondary ones. This includes the cost of supervisory officers and their administrative support as well as the various technical and clerical functions required to operate school boards.

What are some reasonable benchmarks for the resources required to provide the services described in the previous section?

As stated earlier, the goal of this paper is to attempt to quantify a sufficient level of funding and expenditure. In this section an attempt is made to find some reasonable benchmarks for expenditure.

1. *Physical Facilities*

Suburban growth, aging plant in established communities, developing health and safety issues, plant obsolescence caused by changing teaching methods, these are all factors which require a continuous replenishment of our school buildings. A thirty year replacement cycle would require new or refurbished places for about 70,000 students a year or about 80 schools per year or approximately $750,000,000 per year. In addition to making schools better places to learn, the systematic renewal of Ontario's schools will result in economies and efficiencies in operation and maintenance. Based on current expenditure rates, the operation and maintenance of schools should add another $1.3 billion for a total of $2.05 billion.

2. *Curricular and other School Materials*

Texts, library books, lab and shop materials and equipment, computers and peripherals, software, etc., are "consumables" which must be replaced on a continuous basis. Eight hundred dollars per student per year or $1.60 billion would purchase one $2,000 computer every four years and $100 per year each of (i) texts and related materials; (ii) lab and shop materials and equipment; and (iii) library books and other research resources per student.

3. Staff

The recent staff reductions in Ontario's education system have increased class size and reduced in-school support such as teaching aids, other para-professionals, clerical and caretaking staff. Board level support staff such as computer technicians, psychometrists, psychologists and curriculum specialists have also been cut. Like the loss of teachers, these staff losses diminish the educational opportunities for students. Before these staff cuts, in 1992, Ontario school boards had an average of 96 employees of all kinds for every 1,000 students. By 1994 the number had fallen to 92 employees per thousand. By contrast, the number of school district employees per 1,000 students was, in the most recent data, 111 employees per thousand students in the average U.S. state. Increasing the Ontario school board employee rate to the U.S. state average would (i) provide additional teachers to lower class size and provide additional special education services; and (ii) add additional support staff at the school and board level. This 21% increase in staff would increase the staff cost (salaries and benefits) not accounted for elsewhere to approximately $11.2 billion.

4. *Central Administration and Pupil Transportation*

This paper proposes to retain the current level of expenditure for these two functions or about $1.0 billion.

5. *Summary of proposed school board expenditures for the operation of the regular elementary and secondary school programme.*

Plant	$2.05 billion
Learning Materials	$1.60 billion
Staff	$11.20 billion
Central Admin. & Transportation	$1.00 billion
Total Board Expenditure For Day School Programmes	$15.85 billion

The elementary/secondary portion of the MET internal budget would not be included in this amount.

This would correspond to approximately $7,900 per pupil per year. Adding an additional $500 per pupil for MET based expenditures would bring the total to $8,400 per year. Based on the data from Statistics Canada compiled by the Canadian Teachers' Federation for the 1995–6 school year, this would give Ontario the third highest per pupil expenditure – ahead of the other provinces and behind the two territories. This is not unreasonable given that the personal income per capita in Ontario is the highest of the Canadian provinces. When compared to the U.S., this expenditure would approach the U.S. average of $8,410 and be less than the values in adjacent states like New York ($12,596) or Michigan ($9,915).

One obvious consequence of the lower spending levels in Ontario schools is the lower staffing ratios and higher pupil to classroom teacher ratios noted earlier in this paper. The higher per pupil expenditures advocated in this paper are intended – for the most part – to address this deficiency in Ontario's schools.

6. *Other School Funding Issues*
   a) Adult Education in Day Schools

   In 1996 there were approximately 26,000 adults enrolled in regular day school or day school continuing education programmes. At present, the grant system presumes that $2,257 per pupil is sufficient to fund the education of students who are age twenty-one and older. That level of funding denies adult students educational opportunities equivalent to those available to younger students and is thus blatant age discrimination. Not only is it unfair, it is also unwise. The economic gain from an investment in these returning adults is as great – if not greater than the return on the investment in the younger students.

Funding these students at the same level as those under twenty-one would increase the day school expenditure by approximately 1.4% or $220 million.

b) Evening and Summer Continuing Education

When the continuing education grant of $2,257 per full time equivalent student was established, it was recognized that these programmes used facilities – buildings, equipment, texts, labs, curriculum, etc. – which had been purchased for the regular day school programme and which were available for use for the continuing education programme without much additional cost. This figure was set some years ago and does not reflect rising costs since then. Given the funding assumptions, a figure of 70% of the day school expenditure or $5,530 would be more realistic today. This would add approximately $370 million to the current $150 million cost of such credit programmes.

c) Coping with Rapid Change

As measured by outcomes, Ontario's elementary and secondary education system is one of the best in the world. Various national and international studies have demonstrated Ontario's leadership in student retention, the avoidance of gender bias, graduation rates, secondary to post-secondary transition and post-secondary success rates. In other jurisdictions in North America, the qualifications of a person with an Ontario education is readily accepted. Finally, despite the poverty of workplace training, Ontario has one of the world's most highly skilled workforce – a workforce that can learn how to learn.

Ontario's schools must, however, reach beyond their present successes to reach new levels of accomplishment – both for the individual student and for society as a whole. There may be little room in our society for those without significant literacy skills. The economic wellbeing of the province may come to depend not on geography or natural resources but on the ability of its residents to manipulate ideas and information. It would be wise, therefore, to invest additional sums to meet these new challenges. We would propose a $1.0 billion annual *Investment for Tomorrow Fund* which would be disbursed in the following way:

- $500 million *Equal Opportunity Fund.* These funds would be targeted to the 5% of the student population most at risk. Funds would be used to provide the additional resources required to help them succeed.
- $400 million *Adapting to Change Fund.* These funds would be used by school boards to develop and implement curriculum to meet the new expectations. The fund would cover the purchase of new learning materials, texts, etc. and the re-training and upgrading of teachers and other educational workers.
- $100 million *Infrastructure Fund.* These funds would be used by school boards to renovate existing schools so that the new teaching and learning technologies may be used in those schools. Intended uses of the fund would include the reconstruction of learning areas and re-cabling of schools for information networks and internet access.

7. *Total funding requirements*

In the first part of this section, an attempt was made to identify a sufficient level of funding to meet the needs of elementary and secondary schools. The amount arrived at was $15.85 billion or $7,900 per student. In addition, other funding issues have been identified which, if addressed, would require funding above that level. These are:

- Adult Education $220 million
- Other Continuing Education $370 million
- Investment For Tomorrow $1.00 billion

Depending on whether some, or all of these additional expenditures are made, the total requirement for schools ranges between $15.85 and $17.44 billion.

How should Ontario's elementary and secondary education system be funded?

The provincial share of the cost should be large enough that its contribution can assure both adequacy and equity. If the Ontario government were to underwrite 60% of the $15.85 to $17.44 billion – bringing its contribution rate back to where it was twenty years ago – its share would be $9.5 to $10.5 billion, somewhat more than two and a half times the current (1997) $3.9 billion. If the other areas of the province's expenditure budget were to remain unchanged, this school grant would amount to approximately 15% to 17% of the Ontario government budget – about what school grants were in the 1970s. If this course were taken, local taxes would fall from $7.6 billion to $6.4 or $6.9 billion.

How should Ontario's funding model assure equity?

First, the larger provincial share and the higher average per pupil amount will reduce the importance of the inevitable local variations in taxing wealth. Second, the grant funding categories should follow two broad principles: (i) equal treatment of equals or horizontal equity; and (ii) unequal – but equitable – treatment of unequals or vertical equity. Horizontal equity requires that all students have access to the level of funding required to provide the same base level of service. Vertical equity requires that: (a) additional funds be provided where costs for the same services are higher; and (b) additional funds be provided where additional or high cost programmes are required to meet the basic educational needs.

Horizontal equity should be provided for in the base level of funding. Vertical equity should be provided for in additional grants to meet identified needs and costs due to factors such as population sparsity, poverty, multiple languages of instruction, constitutional entrenchments, the distance from urban centres and the higher costs associated with education in the urban core.

These principles were manifest in the current (1996) General Legislative Grant (GLG) regulations. Unfortunately, the implementation of those concepts was hindered by several developments. First, the per pupil disbursements were driven, not by need, but by the total funds available from the Treasurer and the estimated enrolment. The second problem was that the GLG regulations failed to recognize the additional costs and additional program requirements associated with the core of large urban areas. The final difficulty was that the data used to allocate compensatory amounts was often hopelessly out of date.

If student equity is to be achieved in a new funding model, these three difficulties – inadequate funding levels, insensitive equalizing models and old data – must be overcome.

Conclusion

This paper advocates raising the average per pupil expenditure of Ontario's school boards to a range between $7,900 and $8,400 – depending on the options chosen. This would bring Ontario's expenditures into line with other North American jurisdictions – particularly the American ones – which recognize that individual and community prosperity depends upon the education of our citizens. If, as this paper recommends, 60% of this increased level of funding came from provincial government revenues, grants to schools would consume – all other things being equal – about the same proportion of the Ontario government budget as those grants did in 1975.

Appendix 1

A Comparison of American and Canadian Per Pupil Expenditures
American Data From The National Education Association
Canadian Data From The Canadian Teachers Federation
Currency Conversion US$1.00 = CAN$1.30

Rank	Jurisdiction	Per Pupil Expenditures US$
1	Yukon Territory	$13,102
2	NWT	11,267
3	New Jersey	9,735
4	New York	9,689
5	Alaska	9,100
6	Connecticut	8,991
7	Delaware	7,644
8	Michigan	7,627
9	Rhode Island	7,333
10	Massachusetts	7,241
11	Dist. of Columbia	7,224
12	Wisconsin	7,201
13	Maryland	7,186
14	Minnesota	7,141
15	Pennsylvania	7,139
16	Vermont	7,122
17	West Virginia	7,120
18	New Mexico	6,845
19	Iowa	6,806
20	Hawaii	6,800
21	Oregon	6,794
22	Florida	6,740
23	Indiana	6,738
24	Maine	6,595
25	New Hampshire	6,484
26	Wyoming	6,347
27	Ohio	6,311
28	Nevada	6,252
29	Colorado	6,250
30	Virginia	6,173

Rank	Jurisdiction	Per Pupil Expenditures US$
31	Illinois	5,950
32	Kansas	5,940
33	Kentucky	5,924
34	Texas	5,871
35	Nebraska	5,740
36	Georgia	5,734
37	Montana	5,734
38	Washington	5,708
39	Quebec	5,638
40	California	5,544
41	Manitoba	5,475
42	Missouri	5,417
43	British Columbia	5,412
44	Arizona	5,377
45	South Dakota	5,361
46	**Ontario**	**5,355**
47	South Carolina	5,328
48	North Carolina	5,189
49	Alabama	5,020
50	North Dakota	4,960
51	Oklahoma	4,932
52	Louisiana	4,899
53	Idaho	4,765
54	Arkansas	4,720
55	Tennessee	4,572
56	Utah	4,496
57	Saskatchewan	4,472
58	New Brunswick	4,444
59	Mississippi	4,413
60	Alberta	4,402
61	Newfoundland	4,222
62	Nova Scotia	4,189
63	PEI	3,782

US Average $6,469
Canadian Average $5,228

Source: Table compiled by J. McEwen from data supplied by the Canadian Teachers' Federation and the National Education Association and validated by Infometrica.

Appendix 2

A Comparison of Ontario's Position in the Canadian Provinces in Terms of Personal Income and Local Provincial Revenues

		YEAR 1985	1990	1995
Per Capita Personal Income	Amount	16,739	23,113	24,011
	Rank	2	1	1
Per Capita Local/ Provincial Gov't Revenues	Amount	4,150	6,275	6,457
	Rank	5	5	10

Ontario has long been one of, if not the, wealthiest province in Canada. The table above shows that in 1985 Ontario ranked second – behind Alberta – in personal income per capita. In 1990 and again in 1995, the personal income per capita was the highest of the Canadian provinces.

Despite the higher levels of income in Ontario, revenues flowing to the provincial and local governments have, when expressed on a per capita basis, been less than what was raised in many other provinces. Thirty years ago Ontario's per capita local/provincial revenues were third highest in the Canadian provinces. In 1975, in 1985 and again in 1990 Ontario ranked fifth among the provinces. By 1995 Ontario – still the province with the highest incomes – had sunk to tenth place.

Appendix 3

Classroom Teacher To Pupil Ratio 1994–1995 Estimates

Rank	State	Ptr	Rank	State	Ptr
	United States	17.1	6	Nebraska	14.5
1	Vermont	12.5	7	Connecticut	14.6
2	Dist. of Col.	13.1	8	Virginia	14.7
3	New Jersey	13.6	9	West Virginia	14.8
4	Maine	14.0	10	North Dakota	14.9
5	Massachusetts	14.3	11	Arkansas	15.0
12	South Dakota	15.	35	Minnesota	17.4

Rank	State	Ptr	Rank	State	Ptr
13	Texas	15.1	36	Pennsylvania	17.4
14	Virgin Islands	15.1	37	Indiana	17.5
15	Kansas	15.1	38	Ohio	17.6
16	New York	15.1	39	Maryland	17.6
17	Wyoming	15.2	40	Alabama	17.6
18	Wisconsin	15.3	41	Tennessee	17.7
19	Oklahoma	15.3	42	Mississippi	17.8
20	Missouri	15.3	43	Hawaii	17.9
21	Puerto Rico	15.5	44	Amer. Samoa	18.3
22	Iowa	15.6	**45**	**Ontario**	**18.5**
23	New Hampshire	15.9	46	Colorado	18.5
24	North Carolina	16.4	47	North Marian	18.7
25	Georgia	16.4	48	Nevada	18.9
26	Montana	16.5	49	Idaho	19.5
27	South Carolina	16.5	49	Michigan	19.9
28	Delaware	16.6	50	Oregon	19.9
29	Louisiana	16.6	51	Washington	20.2
30	Florida	16.7	52	Rhode Island	21.0
31	Alaska	16.8	53	Arizona	21.1
32	Illinois	17	54	Utah	21.6
33	Kentucky	17.3	55	California	24.1
34	New Mexico	17.3	56	Guam	32.2

Source: U.S. Department of Education, NCEs, Common Core of Data

Source For Ontario: MET Data

Chapter Six

POST SECONDARY EDUCATION: AN ALTERNATIVE VISION

Introduction

The Harris government views postsecondary education as it views elementary and secondary education, the health care system, and other vital programs: through the myopic vision of a "business paradigm." According to this paradigm, responsiveness and accountability to the needs of the market and the private sector are central features in defining a competent postsecondary system. In such a view, change is effective only if it aids in bringing about a postsecondary system more in tune with the shifting needs of the private sector. Excellence is narrowly defined by Education Minister John Snobelen as helping "meet employer and work force requirements for well-educated and well-trained graduates and high-quality research; and [helping] make Ontario more competitive internationally in all fields of endeavour."[1]

In July 1996, the Minister appointed an Advisory Panel to consult with the postsecondary community and the public on the future of higher education in Ontario. The panel was comprised of five administrators from the postsecondary, government, and private sectors. There was no representation from students, faculty, or employee groups. Consultation was hurried, and limited to roundtable discussions with campus delegations that were hand-picked by university administrators. The Advisory Panel's report, released in December 1996, was a huge disappointment to many in the postsecondary community.

The Panel did recognize the destructive impact of a decade of under-funding of higher education, and it recommended an increase in government contributions to the operating grants of universities and colleges in order to bring Ontario up to the national average. It also recommended the development of a research policy for the province and extra funding for research infrastructure. While these recommendations reflected the overwhelming call for government re-investment in higher education, they were contradicted by the rest of the report's recommendations. Despite the unanimous condemnation of deregulation, corporatisation and privatization by faculty, staff, and students during the consultation process, the Panel recommended the deregulation of tuition fees, increased corporate involvement in education, and the opening up of the system to private institutions. These and other measures would all lead to two-tiered higher education in Ontario – a vision of postsecondary education very much in line with the vision of the Minister of Education and Training.

The Postsecondary Education Working Group is a coalition of student, faculty, and support staff representatives. We believe that there is a need to develop and articulate an alternative vision for postsecondary education in Ontario. Our objections to the Minister's method of measuring excellence are two-fold. Firstly, its narrow focus on short-term needs places undesirable and dangerous restrictions on the work conducted by universities and colleges. Secondly, it contradicts the mandates and guidelines established to ensure a publicly-funded system of higher learning governed by the principles of quality and accessibility. In fact, the variety of programs offered at postsecondary institutions in Ontario, and the broad range of options available to students, might actually be a better means for achieving the needs of industry and the private sector in the long term (compared to the short-run cost-cutting and deregulation envisioned by John Snobelen). However, postsecondary education does much more than that – it also enhances the cultural and social life of the province and its citizens.

This paper is designed to generate discussion about the preferred direction of postsecondary education in Ontario that can eventually be reflected in the Ontario Alternative Budget.

Starting Points: Principles for Postsecondary Education in Ontario

The Postsecondary Education Working Group believes that education in Ontario should be guided by the following principles and goals:

a) education as a right of citizenship;

b) high-quality education at all levels and in all types of postsecondary education;

c) removal of financial barriers for postsecondary education;

d) academic freedom and pluralism in postsecondary education;

e) fair and equitable working conditions for all persons employed in postsecondary education;

f) education equity and employment equity at postsecondary institutions;

g) educational programs and services that address regional disparities and recognize the diverse needs of Ontario's population;

h) support for scholarly research in recognition that this research is essential to higher education and to the social and economic welfare of the province;

i) the delivery of public higher education primarily through public funding, in recognition that the principal benefit of postsecondary education is to society;

j) opposition to the commercialization and privatization of postsecondary educational programs and services;

k) the shared financial responsibility of the federal government and the provinces for postsecondary education, training, and student aid;

l) increased funding for postsecondary education by both levels of government.

Funding

The current government has stated that "over the years Ontario's public postsecondary educational institutions have served us well." Measured on such terms as the quality of education and research, responsiveness to student and community needs, and international recognition, Ontario's colleges and universities have proved invaluable in meeting the social, cultural and economic needs of the province.

Essential to an excellent system of public higher education is adequate government funding. However, in the last decade or so, universities and colleges have faced diminishing resources and inadequate financial input from all levels of government. Ontario now has one of the most poorly funded systems of higher education in North America. In the university sector, Council of Ontario Universities' (COU) statistics dramatically demonstrate the current funding crisis. Over the past decade, the universities share of Ontario government spending has declined from 6% to 3% of the total, while full-time equivalent enrolment has grown by nearly 37%. The loss in government grants has meant a 38% reduction in funding per student. In the college system, funding per student has dropped by 42% since 1989. Compared to the level of government investment in other provinces, Ontario now ranks last.

A recent COU economic study shows that a 20% reduction in provincial grants to universities would save the government $376 million – but the estimated negative spinoff effect for business would reduce total sales by $1 billion and would reduce tax revenues, for the three levels of government, by $317 million. Directly and indirectly, some 14,550 jobs would also be lost. Cuts to college funding would also have a disproportionate and negative impact. Yet this year, the Ontario government made the largest single cut to the funding allocations of universities and colleges. In constant dollar terms, the $400 million cut translates to approximately a 17% decline in revenue for postsecondary institutions.

The impact of this financial situation for the quality of postsecondary education must also be taken into account. Most colleges and universities are now operating with diminished faculty and support-staff complements. Hiring freezes, layoffs and attrition constitute the norm across the province. Class sizes have grown significantly, resulting in less interaction between students and their instructors, while educational choices have been sharply curtailed by a host of course and program cancellations. Libraries do not have the funds to maintain book holdings at needed levels. Diminished funding has not only eroded university research infrastructure but threatens the ability of Ontario universities to conduct the type of research that has sustained their national and international reputations and teaching quality. Underfunding has also impeded cooperation among institutions and created an unhealthy "turf war" in which institutions point fingers at one another in their efforts to minimize the impact on their own funding.

Building repairs cannot be made, or are delayed, posing health and safety threats. Equipment is out of date, affecting both the quality of students' education and the quality of research – as well as risking the health and safety of students and staff that use the equipment. In 1993, the estimated value of deferred maintenance for universities was about $522 million. And it can only get worse; most campus buildings were constructed in the 1960s and 1970s and are now starting to erode. The annual maintenance costs of university facilities is estimated to be about $130 million;

over the next decade the deferred maintenance problem will grow to unmanageable proportions. For the college system, current deferred maintenance is approximately $204 million. The current replacement value of all college facilities in the province is estimated at about $3.59 billion. If not addressed, the deferred maintenance of Ontario's colleges is likely to grow to $755 million after 10 years, and $2.8 billion after 20 years.

Funding for postsecondary education should be regarded primarily as a public responsibility in recognition that the principal benefits of higher education are to society as a whole. A 1995 survey conducted for the federal Department of Finance revealed that a majority of Canadians rejected cuts to federal and provincial support for higher education. Almost 60% of those surveyed preferred higher taxes or a budget deficit to reductions in postsecondary education funding.

The Ontario government should increase the public's investment in postsecondary education in order to maintain the quality and accessibility of higher education in the province. In order to bring the government contribution to our postsecondary system up to the national average, the government would need to increase funding by $485 million. Further funding should address the operating, capital and research needs of the system. Funding allocations should be made on a multi-year basis to ensure stability.

Accessibility

The Postsecondary Education Working Group is committed to universal accessibility to postsecondary education in Ontario. A society which aspires to overcome social and economic inequality must provide educational opportunities which break social barriers and bypass economic disadvantages. Foremost in our concerns regarding universal accessibility is our belief that a prospective student's inability to finance his/her education should never prevent access. Economic barriers such as high tuition fees, inadequate student aid programs, the lack of decent summer jobs, and other costs associated directly with achieving a postsecondary education can all play a part in restricting access.

Accessibility means more than overcoming social and economic barriers to postsecondary education. For example, there are prospective students who are denied access to higher education because of the geographical unavailability of a college or university, or in the case of full-time employees, the geographical unavailability of a part-time studies program. As such, our concept of accessibility also encompasses the geographic dispersal of higher education facilities offering a broad range of programs throughout the province.

Tuition Fees

Given that tuition fees constitute the largest education-related expense, it comes as no surprise that they also pose one of the most formidable economic barriers facing students. By all indications, tuition fees in Ontario have far exceeded the threshold at which they become a barrier to accessibility for students from lower and even middle income backgrounds. Recent years have seen massive increases in tuition fees in Ontario. University tuition has increased 140% in the last decade, and college fees have gone up 90% since 1990. The Harris government has implemented the largest single-year tuition increases in the province's history – 20% for university students and 15% for college students in 1996/97 and 10% (up to 20% in some programs) in 1997/98. These increases have occurred at the same time as family incomes and savings rates have dropped, and youth unemployment rates have skyrocketed.

There has never really been a clear policy on tuition in Ontario. Tuition levels have largely depended on the government's willingness or unwillingness to fund postsecondary institutions. As government funds have been cut back in recent years, students have been forced to fill the gap. And as universities and colleges become more strapped for funds, administrators are calling for more "flexibility" in setting fees – in order to "extract profit" from particular programs. In essence,

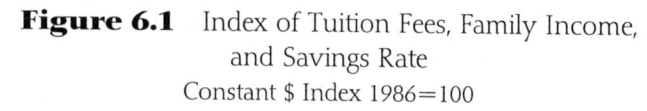

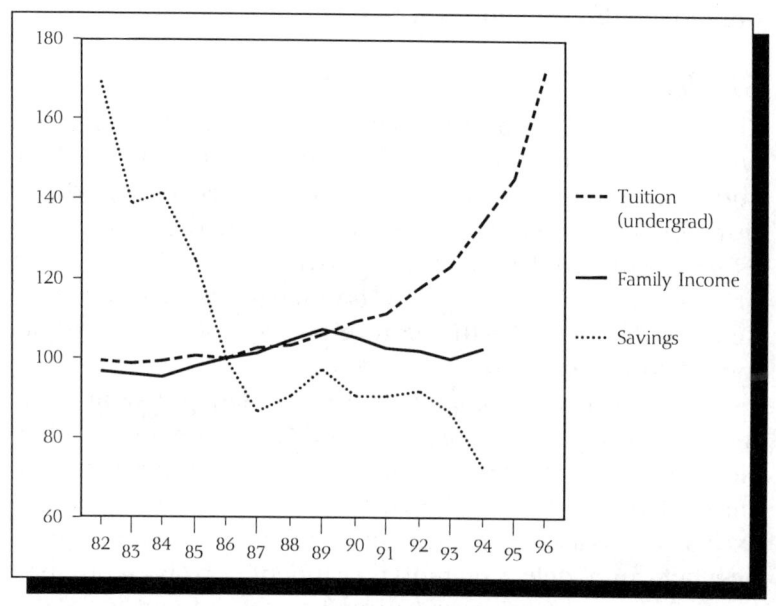

Figure 6.1 Index of Tuition Fees, Family Income, and Savings Rate
Constant $ Index 1986=100

administrators want to be given permission to maintain postsecondary education funding through massive increases in tuition. The government's Advisory Panel responded to administrators' lobbying by recommending the full deregulation of tuition fees. As the Harris government has already deregulated fees for international students and dentistry programs, it is likely that the Ministry will follow through with this recommendation. This will limit access to the more expensive programs and institutions to those that can afford to pay, or to those who are willing to risk massive debt.

Any further increases in tuition, especially of the kind associated with deregulation or a wholesale restructuring of the cost-sharing paradigm of postsecondary education, are bound to have devastating ramifications on the participation rates of lower income students, and hence on the socio-economic make-up of the student population. As it stands, we are already not far from a system in which ability to pay outweighs all other considerations in determining Ontario's future postsecondary students. These future changes can only make the situation worse.

Student Aid

There is a need for a revamped student assistance program which reflects the real costs associated with being a student, and which guarantees accessibility of postsecondary education. Even in a strictly economic sense, the immediate expenses incurred in such an undertaking will more than pay off in the long run with graduates who are less burdened with debt and therefore more capable of contributing to Ontario's economy.

There are several components to a student aid system; the two main components are grants and loans. Ontario's student aid system placed a high emphasis on grants until they were eliminated in 1993/94. The current system, OSAP, is almost exclusively loans-based, with the possibility of loan forgiveness (a form of deferred grant) if a student borrows more than a certain amount per year (currently, that amount is $7,000). There are bursaries available to students with disabilities. Eligibility for the loans is determined by a number of factors: the cost of the program, incomes of the students' parents or spouse, number of dependents, assets, summer earnings, part-time employment, other income, etc. Repayment at a fixed monthly rate begins six months after graduation; interest relief exists as long as a student remains registered.

There are a number of ways the system could be reformed. The Postsecondary Education Working Group will be looking at some of these options, including expanding the grants system to reinstate child-care bursaries, and providing grants to other traditionally-marginalized groups. The Harris government is determined to replace OSAP with an Income Contingent Repayment Plan (ICRP) – a plan that is popular among financial institutions, the editorial writers of the *Globe and Mail*, and the government's Advisory Panel. ICRPs have been abandoned by other provinces, and have been demonstrated to be costly to both students and governments – they increase debt loads, lengthen repayment periods (thereby increasing the amount of interest accrued), and require tremendous administrative costs. While ICRPs do allow a graduate to repay their loan at a rate geared to their income, they do not reduce the overall amount of debt (in fact, for individuals with low or middle incomes, the amount of debt *increases* as the interest compounds over the 25–30 years of repayment). If tied to tuition increases, ICRPs would effectively close the doors to higher education for many students.

Educational Equity

Both universities and colleges are experiencing an increase in the number of students returning from the workforce to undertake further education and training and to upgrade their skills, knowledge, and accreditation. Our postsecondary system must recognize the increasing diversity of its student population. The transition from the workforce to higher education can be difficult, and many adult learners require additional services or remedial upgrading. In addition, remedial courses or English as a Second Language programs are necessary to ensure the success of students who may be new to Canada.

Staffing

Excellence in postsecondary teaching, research and services is directly related to the quality and number of academic and non-academic staff in Ontario's universities and colleges. Government funding cutbacks have resulted in significant loss of staff. In the university sector, the Council of Ontario Universities has noted that the full-time faculty complement shrank by 1,055 and full-time non-academic staff by 1,142 since 1990. During the same time, full-time enrolment has increased by more than 8,000 students. In the college sector, full-time faculty and support staff employment has decreased by about 12% in the past year alone. Full-time staffing levels have continuously declined over the past 6 years. The government's own Advisory Panel on Postsecondary Education has pointed out that universities and colleges are having problems keeping or attracting talented faculty due to deteriorating working conditions, research support and compensation. Attrition is also a problem – faculty are retiring at an alarming rate, but are being replaced only by short-term, part-time contract instructors. This is a huge problem for younger academics or recent graduates, who, if they can not secure stable employment in Ontario, will be forced to leave the province or even the country. They also face deteriorating work conditions that add to the decline in the quality of education.

Loss of staff has eroded the quality and viability of academic programs and services. Class sizes are increasing and student contact with teachers has diminished. The ability of colleges and universities to respond to student interests and needs has been impaired by a reduction in the range of courses and programs offered. Services ranging from building maintenance to student counselling and administrative, technical and library support have been cut back. These changes are not conducive to effective teaching or learning.

Research

Research at postsecondary institutions makes a major contribution to Ontario's social, cultural and economic development, and is an integral part of higher education. Investment in research is fundamental to keeping the province competitive in a global economy. It is widely recognized that Canada spends far less per capita on research and development than almost every European country, and half as much as the United States and Japan. Moreover, Canada relies on its universities to perform over a quarter of its research, far more than all of our major competitors.

The Harris government seems to view research in a restrictive manner, as having a narrow economic function and importance, and concentrated in the basic and applied sciences. In fact, research carried out in the humanities, social sciences, and natural sciences all have the potential for increasing basic knowledge and for producing social, economic, and technological breakthroughs in a way that is relevant and readily available to society as a whole.

Private sector funding for university research is small, and limited to funding for projects that will directly benefit the corporate donor. The largest source of funding for university research comes from the Federal Research Granting Councils which provided Ontario universities with more than a quarter of a billion dollars in 1994. However, as noted by the Council of Ontario Universities, the proportion of federal grants received by Ontario universities has declined from 42% of the national total just over a decade ago to 36% now. This is less than Ontario's share on a per capita basis. Each 1% loss represents almost $10 million of lost income annually.

The Ontario government's Advisory Panel on Postsecondary Education has pointed out that one of the greatest obstacles to the research competitiveness of Ontario universities is the difficulty of supporting and maintaining both the intellectual and material infrastructure. The provincial government's failure to provide Ontario universities with sufficient funding to build and maintain labs, equipment, libraries and other research facilities has made it difficult for universities to compete for sponsored research. The loss of experienced faculty who are able to attract research dollars has also limited universities' ability to obtain federal funding. In addition, diminished research capacity means that graduate students – future researchers – do not receive the opportunities, support, supervision, and training they require. The lack of an explicit and coordinated government research policy has further impeded the research competitiveness of Ontario universities. Most damaging of all to the universities' capacity to carry out research, however, is the failure of the provincial government to provide adequate operating grants to universities to fund state-of-the-art infrastructure and retain the number and calibre of faculty this province needs to innovate, grow and be competitive.

Accountability

Accountability is essential to the delivery of excellent postsecondary education. First and foremost, as public institutions, our universities and colleges are accountable to society, and therefore their priorities and mandates must always take into account society's needs and not merely a narrow cost-benefit analysis.

Currently, there are mechanisms in place at several levels to ensure accountability. At the system-wide level, colleges are governed by the Council of Regents, which consists of government appointees. The College Standards and Accreditation Council functioned to establish consistent standards amongst college programs, but was recently taken over by the Ministry of Education and Training. Universities do not have a system-wide governing body, but there are system-wide mechanisms in place, including accrediting bodies like the Ontario Council on Graduate Studies, which reviews graduate programs, and regular external reviews of academic programs, departments, etc. The Ontario Council on University Affairs, which functioned as an advisory body on academic issues, was eliminated by the Harris government in 1996.

At the institutional level, accountability is the responsibility of university committees, academic councils or Senates, and Boards of Governors. Unfortunately, these extensive mechanisms often exclude effective participation from major stakeholders in the postsecondary community. Boards of Governors, which have the most control over the direction of an institution and its budget, are dominated by representatives from the private sector with a vested interest in the erosion of our public postsecondary system.

The postsecondary education sector is a unique community in which professionals, academics, students and staff interact with each other in a collegial manner. Public participation and input into this community are essential, as the postsecondary community's members are drawn from all levels of Ontario's society. As such it is imperative that no single group be allowed to have a level of influence over accountability mechanisms that will override the concerns of others. Effective mechanisms of accountability for our postsecondary sector must be open, transparent, democratic, and provide significant representation to all stakeholder groups.

Technology

While not as prevalent as in some areas, technological applications have already had an impact on postsecondary education in Ontario. Unfortunately, the piecemeal approach to technological change witnessed so far has been a far-from-adequate response to the issue of technology in our schools. Where technological applications exist, they have so far been inadequate replacements for current pedagogical methods, and have had more to do with cost-cutting than improving quality.

We are not confident that the current political climate in Ontario will be conducive to reversing this trend; indeed, all indications are that there will be an increase in the proliferation of distance education methods and practices, with more and more courses and programs delivered entirely via information and communication technologies. We must step out of the cost-saving paradigm and view technological change in light of its effects on the quality and accessibility of postsecondary education. Technology can serve to complement, but not replace, the myriad interactions that presently occur on campuses across Ontario. Such a use of technology is neither cheap nor easily installed, but it is the only way to ensure that students in Ontario receive both technologically advanced and high-quality educational programs, and that instructors and staff can develop and use the technology in ways that are conducive to effective learning.

Endnote

[1] "Future Goals for Ontario Colleges and Universities," discussion paper, July 1996.

Chapter Seven

CHILD CARE:
THE CASE FOR REFORM

Ontario's child care system is under unprecedented assault. But even without the harsh and unjustifiable Harris cutbacks, the system faces major structural difficulties. Child care subsidy for low income families is still provided on a welfare basis, through the administration of a means test. For moderate and middle-income parents, full-fee child care is quite simply unaffordable. Fees are in the range of up to $12,000 per year per child. Since June, 1995, Ontario has lost 9,500 child care spaces and 26,000 junior kindergarten spaces. Capital spending for junior kindergarten and child care has been eliminated. Flatlined or decreased capital and operating spending leaves absolutely no hope of recovery or future expansion. Cuts to these services for families and children decrease the number of quality care and education options for children, limit their parents' (most often their mother's) ability to work, and erode good, public sector jobs – almost 1,500 mainly female teachers have lost their jobs in junior kindergarten alone.

It is time to implement a new kind of service for young children and their families – a high-quality service that is accessible and affordable so that families have genuine child-care options. Ontario could spend more and could spend differently by combining care and education into a full-day program for over three year-olds, while stabilizing funding for child care for the under-threes. In addition, the province should work with the federal government to provide well-paid, year-long maternity and parental leaves after a child is born.

A reformed early childhood education and care system would help restore economic growth by creating jobs, by creating conditions that allow all Ontarians to participate in the economy, and by enhancing our education system. It should be a major part of the new investment in public services that will contribute to Ontario's revitalization.

Rationale for Reform

There are a number of very sound educational, social and economic reasons to reform and expand our education and care for young children. Whether mothers should or will work outside the home is no longer in question – most do. Over 80% of women with children under the age of 12 are in the paid workforce, either full or part-time, and hence require care for their children during working hours.

Investment in this area will help fight unemployment. The early childhood education sector is highly labour-intensive, and therefore a major source of jobs. In addition, private sector jobs are created in the industries that serve the sector.

Early childhood education can support school achievement. For example, there is evidence, validated by Ontario's Royal Commission on Education, that children in countries with publicly-funded early childhood education from age three are better readers. While all children benefit from high-quality early childhood education programs, these programs are particularly effective in improving the progress and life chances of children who are at risk due to poverty and other reasons.

Availability of early childhood education and care is crucial in eliminating child poverty. Countries that have both universal early childhood services and universal family allowance have much lower rates of child poverty. Availability of early childhood services makes it possible for parents to participate in the paid workforce – ideally a more remunerative option than social assistance. Availability of family allowance recognizes the costs of raising children in all families and provides low income families with an income foundation and financial flexibility.

Steps to Creating Coherent Early Childhood Education and Care

1) *The Early Years' Program and Child Care Funding Reform*

The Early Years Program is a publicly-funded early education and care program for 3–5 year-olds. Parents who decide to use the program may choose to send their children for a half, full or extended day. The program would be voluntary; the statutory school age will not change.

Funding reform would address issues of program stability and affordability for parents. New funding measures would apply to regulated child care for 0–3 year-olds, extended day programs for EYP, before and after school programs for 6–12 year-olds and regulated home child care. Fees would not be a barrier to program access. They would be assessed on a sliding scale: families with income under $25,000/year would pay nothing or a nominal fee, those between $25,000 and $60,000 would pay gradually increasing fees, those with incomes of above $60,000 would pay a maximum fee which reflects the existing universal subsidy for wage enhancement.

Co-ordinated staffing and training could combine and enhance the qualifications of the two professional groups that now work with young children. They could work in teams with two types of qualifications. The Early Years Specialist (EYS) would be a new dual qualification which upgrades current training in both education and child care sectors. Taking the form of a four or five year degree, it would apply to the lead staff in EYP and the primary grades and would be encouraged for supervisors of child care programs. College-university articulation would be available for holders of the Early Childhood Education (ECE) two-year diploma. The Early Years' Associate (EYA) with an Early Childhood Education diploma would work as a team with the Early Years Specialist in the EYP and either with EYS or as lead in child care centres.

2) Maternal / Parental Leave

Optional leave after birth or adoption will be extended to one year at 75% of income for the first 90 days, and 66% after that date. Birthing mothers will be eligible for leave of up to 18 weeks; the remaining 34 weeks may be used by either parent, to share at their discretion.

3) Funding and Implementation for EYP and child care reform

This new system can be implemented over time – it can be "grown" as resources allow, with the growth of EYP allowing a gradual expansion for 0–2 age groups within the existing number of child care spaces.

System Capacity	Year 1	Year 2	Year 3	Mid Point	End
Child Care	148,000	153,000	157,000	109,700	62,200
JK/K*	261,000	260,000	260,000	126,400	0
EYP	8,400	18,000	26,000	197,000	394,000
Total New $	119.5	164.7	233.9	1,378.3	2,500.5

(Capital and Operating in millions)

* Junior Kindergarten / Kindergarten

Jobs restored or created in the first 3 years:

Child Care   2,625
JK/K*   1,444
EYP 3,250 (1/3 teachers, 2/3 ECE)

* Junior Kindergarten / Kindergarten

In Canada, child care was first established for the children of poor, single mothers. Vestiges of this history remain, in the attitudes of some government officials who are of the view that child care is still a program for a marginalized and politically powerless group. While some progress in funding the service (rather than simply the children of the poor) was made between 1985 and 1995, this has eroded recently.

Education, kindergarten included, was established to serve all children. Although the content and quality of education are often the subject of public debate, education is seen as an essential service by most of the public. A combined program is cost-effective. Kindergarten is less expensive than child care for three, four and five year-olds. Many children attend both programs during the course of the day, thus creating some overlap in resources. Combining the two programs using teamed staffing and a middle ground for staff, child ratios and group sizes creates an efficient, high-quality program that will be more expensive on a per child basis than current kindergartens, but less expensive than child care.

Good child care and kindergarten programs may differ slightly in approach, but both types provide education and care. What was a distinction historically has, in the past 25 years, become quite arbitrary. However, kindergarten is the only fully-funded, fully- accessible early childhood education program in Ontario. Attaching the kinds of services needed by today's families (e.g. "wrap-around" care) to this program makes sense. Moving kindergarten out of the school system and attaching it to current child care integrates service but marginalizes our only universal ECE program. Finally, locating early childhood education in schools provides families with one daily stop and an educational continuum until at least age ten.

Early Years Program a Doable Reform

Both the Early Years Program initiative and child care funding reform are urgently needed, yet eminently doable. The proposal set out in this paper permits a phased implementation, which expands as financial resources are made available. The key is getting started, demonstrating that the model works and that an integrated affordable system can be introduced quickly and with relative ease.

Chapter Eight

THE ENVIRONMENT: 'OUR FUTURE, OUR HEALTH'[*]

Introduction

Over the past 18 months, the government of Ontario has undertaken a dismantling of environmental laws, regulations, policies and institutions that is without precedent in the history of the province. We, the member organizations of the Ontario Environmental Protection Working Group, are alarmed about the implications of these changes for the health and well-being of present and future generations of Ontarians. We believe that the future of Ontario's people and its environment is being sacrificed for short-term economic gain.

Ontario citizens have expressed their concern for protection of the natural environment since the early nineteenth century. They created field naturalist clubs throughout the province, which then came together as the Federation of Ontario Naturalists in the early days of this century.

In the post-war years, the Ontario government responded to the concerns expressed by Pollution Probe, the Canadian

---

[*] 'Our Future, Our Health' is a report by the Ontario Environmental Protection Group, endorsed by thirteen major environmental organizations and released in March 1997. We are grateful for their permission to include the main body of the report in our document. It has our wholehearted support. The complete document includes the appendices and may be obtained from the Canadian Institute for Environmental Law and Policy at (416) 923-3529.

Environmental Law Association, the Canadian Environmental Law Research Foundation and others. The regulatory regime put in place in the early 1970s dealt with many of the acute threats to human health and the environment posed by toxic substances. In the following decade, measures to address such problems such as acid rain and ozone-layer depletion were also moved forward by governments, industry and environmental NGOs working together to find common ground and put cost-effective solutions in place.

Despite these successes, air and water pollution, and the handling of hazardous wastes still pose threats to the health of Ontario citizens and the other species with whom we share our environment.

It was clear that further action was needed to protect Ontario's environment well before the current government was elected in June 1995. However, the government has moved in the opposite direction. It has weakened, rather than strengthened Ontario's environmental protection system, with the result that Ontario citizens are now exposed to greater environmental risk than they were two years ago.

The province's capacity to address ongoing serious environmental issues is being dismantled. The problems of urban air pollution, the degradation of surface and ground water in southern Ontario, industrial air and water pollution in northern Ontario, and the continued generation of more than two million tonnes of hazardous and liquid industrial wastes each year, have all been highlighted by the Ministry of Environment and Energy itself in its 1992 Status Report on Ontario's Environment.

Moreover, the province's actions are undermining the achievements of the past. These include the reductions of nutrient loadings in the Great Lakes, cuts in acid-rain-causing emissions, and expansion of municipal recycling and household hazardous waste collection programs.

The government's actions are deeply at odds with public opinion regarding environmental protection. Public opinion surveys over the past few years have consistently shown that the public wants stronger, not weaker, government action to protect the environment. An Environics Research/Environmental Monitor survey, completed last summer, for example, indicated that even in the context of budgetary reductions, over 80% of Ontario respondents wanted environmental laws to be made stricter, and 13% favoured maintaining the status quo. Only 3% supported removing some requirements from existing laws.

In this document, we set out an alternative vision of what environmental protection in this province should provide. It focuses on the fundamental role of the provincial government in the protection of public goods, such as public health and safety, clean air, water and land, the protection and conservation of biological diversity, and the ecologically sustainable management of natural resources. The environmental policy debate in Ontario must deal with these real environmental problems which we face as a society, and not just short-term economic concerns.

We conclude with a challenge to the Premier and Minister of Environment and Energy asking them to make public commitments to the following measures:

1. **ensure that Ontario is able to fulfil its intergovernmental environmental commitments**, such as those under the *1994 Canada-Ontario Agreement on the Great Lakes Ecosystem*, **and that it does not undermine Canada's international commitments** under such treaties as the *Great Lakes Water Quality Agreement*;
2. **provide detailed annual state of the environment reports to Ontarians**; and
3. **provide for the effective enforcement of Ontario's laws which protect the environment and the health and safety of its residents.**

These steps are essential. These commitments must be made to protect the health and well-being of present and future generations of Ontarians.

Serious Ecological Health Problems Continue to Exist in Ontario

1) Air Pollution

Some of the most serious involuntary health risks to which Ontario citizens are exposed are associated with different forms of air pollution. Many air pollution problems, such as acidification caused by sulphur dioxide emissions, have been significantly reduced by regulatory action taken by Ontario governments over the past two decades.

However, Ontario citizens, particularly those living in urban areas, still face a number of health threats as a result of poor air quality. The pollutants of concern include ground-level ozone, nitrogen oxides, particulates, hydrogen sulphide, sulphur dioxide and toxic substances.

Urban smog, caused by fossil fuel combustion in transportation and stationary energy uses, poses the most significant threat. While concentration levels of some pollutants have declined over the past decade, ground-level ozone concentrations have steadily increased. The Ontario and Canadian governments project that this trend will continue unless additional action is taken. Scientists have documented a causal correlation between hospital admissions for respiratory problems and high smog levels and "between premature death due to respiratory disease and airborne particulates, ozone, and nitrogen oxide."

The smog problem was documented by the Ontario Ministry of Environment and Energy in its 1992 State of the Enviornment Report:

> Ground-level ozone levels have shown a resurgence in the last few years. In places where industry and vehicle traffic are densely concentrated, pollution levels rise rapidly when weather conditions favour their buildup. As a result, many centres in the province continue to experience periodic episodes of moderate to poor air quality.

More recent documentation was provided by the Ministry in its 1996 discussion paper, *Towards a Smog Plan for Ontario*:

It's now well known and documented that smog not only aggravates a wide range of serious health problems such as asthma and other respiratory diseases, it can also increase mortality rates.... Recent studies have linked human death rates with exposure to inhalable particulates. This association is apparent in ambient or open air concentrations typical of metropolitan areas in North America including Toronto, Detroit and Los Angeles.

Dr. Monica Campbell, a toxicologist with the Metro Toronto Teaching Health Units, North York Health Department, has provided this summary of the air pollution threat in Ontario: "Taken together, these studies clearly show that existing pollutant levels in southern Ontario are affecting the public's health." Human health is at risk under existing regulatory programs, even before we begin to experience the effects of the current government's proposals to weaken controls on air pollution.

The smog problem is likely to be seriously affected by a number of the government's actions. These include the repeal of land-use planning policies that were intended to curb urban sprawl and consequent increases in automobile use. The government has also announced its intention to eliminate provincial funding for public transit services in the province. These steps will increase the province's emissions of carbon dioxide, contrary to Canada's and Ontario's international commitment to stabilize CO_2 emissions.

Furthermore, despite the success of the Countdown Acid Rain Program, acid rain deposition continues to be a problem, and further measures will be needed to reduce emissions. In addition, the province's existing standards for a broad range of toxic air pollutants are widely regarded as being out of date and inadequate. In some cases, U.S. and Canadian federal government standards are higher than Ontario standards by several orders of magnitude.

2) *Water Pollution*

Pollution of surface and ground water also poses both direct health threats, from drinking water contamination, and indirect threats as contaminants are passed up the food chain on their way to human consumption. Considerable progress has been made in the province towards reducing some forms of water pollution over the past thirty years. In particular, concentrations of many toxic pollutants have declined, as have phosphorous concentrations in the Great Lakes.

However, the 1992 Ministry of Environment and Energy's Status Report on Ontario's Environment documented the continuing serious water quality problems in the province:

> Problems of nutrient enrichment, turbidity, and bacterial contamination are widespread in inland rivers and lakes across southern Ontario, largely as a result of urban and agricultural land use.
>
> Water with an average faecal coliform density of more than 100 counts per ml in a series of water samples is considered unsafe for swimming or other recreational uses ... levels in excess of this guideline are reached in many parts of southern Ontario....
>
> In general, then these measures of surface water quality, except for phosphorous, have impoved little since the 1970s and in some areas there is evidence of continuing deterioration.

Toxic substances also continue to contaminate Ontario water:

> Because of the potential health risk from eating contaminated fish, sport fish in Ontario's lakes and rivers have been regularly sampled and tested for toxic substances for a number of years. Consumption advisories are issued for those lakes and rivers where contaminated fish have been found ... consumption advisories have been issued for 45–55 cm walleye ... [and] 35–55 cm lake trout ... For both species, total consumption restrictions are relatively few, but partial restrictions are widespread.

The Ministry also noted continuing water quality problems in Northern Ontario, particularly for sensitive areas exposed to acid rain, and due to the local effects of pulp and paper mills, and mining and forestry operations.

In its recent review of environmental protection in Canada, the Organization for Economic Cooperation and Development (OECD) recognized the progress which had been achieved. But it also pointed to continuing problems:

> Surface water quality is generally high and significant improvements have recently been achieved in many locations. Nevertheless, local problems remain: the Great Lakes and St. Lawrence basins continue to suffer from industrial and municipal pollution, urban and agricultural run-off and atmospheric deposition....

The government has proposed a number of measures which are likely to make the problems of surface and groundwater contamination more serious. Among the most significant are the proposals to expand the protection of agricultural activities from the requirements of the province's environmental protection legislation, through amendments to the *Farm Practices Protection Act*. This is despite the growing evidence of the severe impacts of agricultural activities on water quality in the province.

In addition, both the Ministry of Environment and Energy and the Red Tape Commission have proposed to significantly weaken the requirements of the province's MISA (Municipal-Industrial Strategy for Abatement) regulations, which control discharges from industrial sources.

3) Waste Management

The generation and management of hazardous industrial wastes, and non-harzardous municipal solid wastes continue to pose significant problems for Ontario. In its 1992 *Status Report on Ontario's Air, Water and Waste*, the Ministry of Environment and Energy stated that Ontario industries continue to generate approximately 2 million tonnes of hazardous liquid industrial wastes each year. There is evidence that the amount of hazardous liquid industrial waste being shipped off-site for disposal is increasing.

Forty per cent of these wastes are disposed of on-site

through landfilling and discharges to the air, water and municipal sewer systems. Sixty percent is shipped off site for disposal through landfilling, sewage treatment plants, incineration, export, reclamation, and dust suppression.

The Ministry also stated that there were 113,000 tonnes PCBs in storage at 1,751 sites across the province. In addition, it anticipates a need for treatment of 40,000 tonnes of CFC's as these chemicals are phased out. The Ministry highlighted the continuing problems with the disposal of biomedical wastes, particularly in small hospital incinerators which lack modern air pollution equipment, as well.

The Ministry of Environment and Energy and the Red Tape Commission have both proposed major changes to the regulatory regime for the management of hazardous and liquid industrial wastes. Many of these proposed changes would weaken or eliminate many of the existing requirements for the handling of such wastes.

Municipal solid wast management is one area where the Ministry has achieved some significant successes. Its 1992 Status Report claims a 25% reduction in the amount of non-hazardous waste sent to disposal between 1987 and 1992. It also indicates that there has been a dramatic increase in the number of households with access to recycling programs.

However, the successes are also under threat. Funding for municipal recycling and household hazardous waste programs has been eliminated. In addition, the repeal of regulations requiring waste reduction, reuse and recycling measures by Industrial, Commerical and Institutional waste generators, and requiring the use of refillable soft drink containers, have been proposed by the Red Tape Commission.

The Ontario Government is Undermining its Own Capacity to Deal with these Problems

Since taking office in June, 1995, the current government has dismantled many of the tools we need to address these continuing problems. By the 1997/98 fiscal year, the budget of the Ministry of Environment and Energy is to be reduced by 37% against a 1994/95 base year, and the agency is to lose 31% of its staff.

As a result, the Ministry no longer has the capacity to perform many of its core environmental protection functions. This has been made clear by internal Ministry documents recently obtained by the public which indicate growing concern over "regulatory negligence" claims against the Ministry. In effect, the Ministry is taking steps to protect itself from lawsuits from Ontario residents whose persons or property are harmed as a result of the Ministry's inability to carry out its regulatory functions.

Other impacts of the reductions in the Ministry's budget include:

- the number of water monitoring stations has dropped from nearly 700 in 1991 to just over 200;
- the number of air monitoring stations has decreased to its lowest level in twenty years;
- pesticide testing services have been cut by more than half; and
- there has been a significant decline in prosecutions for environmental offenses.

At the same time, the government has amended the *Mining Act*, *Planning Act*, *Environmental Assessment Act*, *Public Lands Act*, *Lakes and Rivers Improvements Act*, *Gasoline Handling Act* and *Conservation Authorities Act* in ways which weaken their environmental protection requirements. Similar amendments to the *Environmental Protection Act* and *Ontario Water Resurces Act* are before the Legislature. Proposals to expand the protection of agricultural activities from the environmental, public health and land-use planning legislation have been presented as well.

The government is also in the process of weakening the regulations passed under these acts which set specific environmental standards. The July 1996 discussion paper *Responsive Environmental Protection* suggested a number of such changes. Many of these proposals, and others put forward by the mining, chemical, petroleum products, waste management and other industry sectors were incorporated into the final report of the Red Tape Review Commission, which was delivered last month. Among other things, the Commission recommended:

- a new definition of "recyclable material" which will remove controls on the movement, handling and storage of hazardous waste materials destined for "recycling";
- the removal of all regulatory controls from on-site waste disposal;
- the elimination of the regulation requiring that some soft-drinks be sold in refillable containers;
- the elimination of the waste reduction, re-use and recycling regulations for industrial, commercial and institutional waste generators;
- the revisions of section 43 of the *Environmental Protection Act* to reduce private sector liability for contaminated lands remediation; and
- the weakening of monitoring and reporting requirements under the province's Municipal-Industrial Strategy for Abatement (MISA) industrial water pollution control program.

Principles for Ontario's Environmental and Natural Resource Policies

We believe that the approaches to environmental protection and natural resources management being pursued by the government of Ontario will cost present and future generations of Ontarians heavily in economic, social and environmental terms.

We believe that a fundamentally different approach, constructed on the following principles, is required to ensure the future well-being of Ontarians.

1. Protecting the Environment

   Ontario's parks, forests, wildlife, air, public lands and waterways constitute a public trust, which must be protected and conserved for the future benefit of all Ontarians.

2. Government Responsibility

   Governments have a fundamental role to play in the protection of these public goods, the protection and enhancement of ecological capital, and in ensuring the environmentally sustainable use of energy, land, material, and water resources. Governments, acting in the public interest, must ensure that economic activities are carried out within the context of sustainability, and are socially desirable and economically viable (on a full cost accounting basis).

3. The Regulatory Framework

   Governments have a responsibility to provide and enforce environmental standards. On the basis of historical experience and current events private actors cannot be relied upon to regulate their own use of public environmental resources. The marketplace alone cannot provide for the effective protection of public goods, such as public health and safety, clean air, water and land, the protection and conservation of biological diversity, and the ecologically sustainable management of natural resources.

4. Public Accountability

   Governments must be able to be held to account for their actions and the consequences of their laws and policies. State of the Environment reporting and public access to information are the cornerstones of this accountability.

5. Public Access to decision-making

   Governments must ensure that those who will be affected by government decisions and policies have the right to participate in the decision and policy-making processes.

6. Resources

Governments must ensure that sufficient resources are provided to agencies, boards and commissions mandated to protect Ontario's environment and natural resources.

We ask that the government of Ontario accept its responsibilities to present and future generations of Ontarians, and act in accordance with these principles.

A Challenge to the Government of Ontario

The Premier of Ontario has made the following public statement regarding the importance of environmental protection:

protecting the environment for the future generations ranks equally with us as the fiscal situation for future generations.

Similarly, the July 1996 Ministry of Environment and Energy consultation paper *Responsive Environmental Protection* stated that:

The fundamental objective of MoEE's regulatory reform is to ensure continued human health and safety and environmental protection while eliminating red tap, obsolete regulations and simplifying the system in order to promote economic growth and job creation.

The paper goes on to say:

There will be no reduction or relaxation of environmental standards as a result of regulatory reform.

Energy Minister, the Hon. Norm Sterling, stated:

I want to ensure that Ontario's high standards are maintained....

His Parliamentary Assistant, Dr. Douglas Galt, M.P.P. for Nothumberland, added:

Improving environmental protection is paramount.

Through these statements, the government of Ontario has indicated its commitment to protecting the health of Ontario citizens and that of all other life in the province. However, this commitment has not been matched by the government's actions.

We have documented here threats to the health of Ontario's environment identified by the Ministry of Environment and Energy and others. We have given examples of actions taken by the Ontario government which significantly reduce its ability to deal with these threats, and in many cases make them worse. We have also documented how many of the government's actions seem likely to undermine Ontario's past environmental successes.

We believe that the interest of future generations of Ontarians can only be protected if the government embarks on a fundamentally different direction with respect to the environment.

As a consequence, we ask the government of Ontario to accept the principles for Ontario's environmental protection and natural resource management policies which we have outlined, and ask that it put these principles into action by making an immediate commitment to take three essential steps.

1) *Fulfilling Intergovermental and International Commitments*

The government's actions raise serious questions about Ontario's ability to fulfil its obligations under a number of major intergovernmental agreements, most notably the *1994 Canada-Ontario Agreement on the Great Lakes Basin Ecosystem*. They treaten Canada's ability to fulfil its obligations under the *Canada-U.S. Great Lakes Water Quality Agreement*. Canada's ability to comply with the requirements of other international agreements, such as the *Canada-U.S. Agreement on Transboundary Air Pollution*, the *Framework Convention of Climate Change*, the *United Nations Convention on Biological Diversity* and the *Montreal Protocol* may be undermined by the province's actions as well.

We ask:

> **that the government commit to ensuring that the Ministry of Environment and Energy, and other relevant Ontario government agencies have the resources and legislative and regulatory means necessary to**

> fulfill its obligations under existing intergovernmental agreements, and that it does not place Canada's ability to comply with international environmental agreements in jeopardy.

2) Reporting on the Quality of Ontario's Environment

The government has claimed that its actions will not weaken the protection of Ontario's environment. It has an obligation to provide Ontarians with the information necessary to verify these claims.

We ask:

> that the government commit to providing Ontarians with a comprehensive annual report on the state of Ontario's environment. This implies that capacity in the areas of environmental monitoring, science, and analysis must be maintained, as must monitoring and reporting requirements for industry under Ontario's environmental legislation.

In the longer term, we suggest that State of the Environment Reporting functions be assigned to the Office of the Environmental Commissioner of Ontario in order to maintain independence and impartiality with regard to this activity.

3) Ensuring the Enforcement of Ontario's Environmental Laws

The reductions in the Ministry's enforcement capacity, and the recent revelation of documents indicating serious concerns regarding the issue of regulatory negligence within the Ministry, raise major questions regarding the continued effective enforcement of Ontario's environmental laws.

We ask:

> that the government commit to ensuring that the MoEE has the capacity and resources to conduct an effective enforcement policy to achieve and maintain province-wide compliance with its legislation and

regulations for the protection of the environment and human health;

that the government commit to providing Ontarians with detailed annual reports on the Ministry's enforcement activities in order to ensure accountability in these areas. These should be modelled on the annual Offenses Against the Environment reports, the last of which was released in 1994; and

that the government provide a commitment that no existing legislative or regulatory requirements for the protection of the environment or human health will be replaced with voluntary, or self-regulatory measures.

We believe that these measures are necessary to ensure the well-being of present and future generations of Ontarians.

Chapter Nine

HEALTH CARE: THE CRISIS CONTINUES

Despite the explicit promises made by Premier Harris during the 1990 election not to cut Medicare or close hospitals, both have been ravaged by his government.

Up to 38 hospitals across Ontario are slated for closure by the Hospital Restructuring Commission. This includes such treasured institutions as Women's College and the Wellesley hospitals in Toronto, as well as smaller community hospitals which remain centres of civic spirit in all parts of the province.

Behind these dramatic acts, which will leave Toronto with the lowest bed-to-people ratio in North America, lies the single Harris imperative: find the cash to pay for the tax cut.

Hospitals have been singled out for a special contribution. A total of $1.3 billion is being squeezed out of their budgets over just three years, at the rate of $365 million in 1996–97, $435 million in 1997–98, and $500 million in 1998–99.

Health Care Download

On January 14, 1997, the government announced its intention to transfer to municipalities 50% of the funding for long term care, 50% funding for social assistance, 100%

funding for public health units, ambulance service, supportive housing and social housing. While they have since backed off the proposal to download long-term care, and are leaving municipalities with "only" 20% of the entire welfare bill, crucial areas of overall health spending remain stretched to the breaking point.

- Home care resources are stretched to the limit. Currently, due to new medical technologies and changing demographics and most importantly the cuts to hospital budgets, the hospital sector is changing its standards for patient care. The result is that people are being sent home from hospital much quicker than they used to be (in some cases 24 hours after surgery). These people still need injections, monitoring, dressings cleaned, etc. And rehabilitation that used to happen in the hospital now happens at home. Often, home care services do not meet current need and the burden either falls to family members or people are re-admitted to hospital because their recovery falters.
- Already the Tories have lowered the standards in nursing homes. They have dropped the requirement for 2.25 minimum hours of care per patient per day.
- It is currently a requirement that municipalities run a home for the aged. Many municipalities have approached the government to drop that requirement. We currently have a mix of profit and non-profit nursing homes and homes for the aged. Most of the non-profits are run by municipalities.
- Public health units are responsible for ensuring the health and safety of a community with inoculations, water quality, environmental health and public health education. The mandatory programs for public health units are currently being re-written in response to the download and the legislation will be amended – lowering standards for public health.
- Ambulance services are provided through a combination

of municipal and private operators. The provincial government funds the system and runs the dispatch. Many feel that provincial funding is necessary in order to avoid boundary disputes and provide seamless service. Some American-based firms have expressed a keen interest in buying up ambulance services. As cash-strapped municipalities face increasing costs the threat of selling off this vital health service becomes more real every day.

The Ontario Alternative Budget Working Group sets out the following basic proposals as an immediate alternative to the present acts of destruction.

1. The Hospital Restructuring Commission should be disbanded.
2. A new, open and democratic health planning process should be created. This planning process would be based upon a firm commitment by the provincial government to maintain the integrity of the health care budget. It should be genuinely inclusive of all sectors of the community, including both health care providers and consumers.
3. The $1.3 billion in hospital funding cuts should be rescinded, and base funding should be restored. There should be a moratorium on further hospital funding cuts.
4. The overall health spending envelope for any local community should not be diminished as the mix of health services delivered by institutions and by community-based agencies is changed by a local health plan.
5. The right of health workers to dignity and fair treatment must be upheld. Health workers are entitled to job security.
6. The down-loading and off-loading of such essential health care services as ambulance services, which are an integral part of the Megacity/Megadump exercise, should be rescinded. Medicare is the responsibility of the provincial government to finance; it does not belong on the property tax.

The first step, as outlined above, is to stop the destruction.

Alternatives

One of the most frequently-heard mantras of neoliberals is that of TINA (**T**here **I**s **N**o **A**lternative). There are alternatives. But the first requirement in building alternatives is to agree on the principle of effective consultation with the people to be served. In this case, it means consultation with the communities, the care-givers and the consumers of health services in all sectors of society. We have tried to tap the knowledge of as many of these groups as possible, in analysing the "official figures" and in coming up with meaningful, though still tentative, alternatives. We count on the consultation and education process that is planned for the coming months, in various parts of Ontario and among various sectors and organizations of the people of Ontario, to sharpen both our knowledge of health problems and the monetary and budgetary figures that make sense.

In that framework, just as our consideration of health problems is related to our commitment to a society based on fairness and social justice, so is our consideration of a health budget related to a fairer tax system that can meet social priorities.

Budget Estimates as Political Tactics

It is so easy to be confused by the profusion of different figures in the Budget Estimates of the Ministry of Health in May, 1997, and in June of the same year, that it is tempting to draw the conclusion that their goal is to sow confusion among their critics.

First, the May figures are grouped, or classified, differently from those of June, and from those of previous years. Comparison is extremely difficult. Money is shifted around between old and new programs, making comparison even more difficult. We have used the figures for the 1997–98 budget, as presented to the Legislative Committee on Estimates, in making our calculations.

In order to be able to assess the claim of the Ministry of Health that it is maintaining health spending at an adequate level, it is necessary to consider a number of key factors.

Population Growth and Inflation

The first of these is population growth and its relation to inflation.

Over the past three years, between 1995 and 1997, inflation has averaged 2.0%, and the cumulative increase in inflation over this time frame totals 6.12%.

During the same period of time, the Ontario population has increased by an average of 1.32%, with a cumulative total of 3.87%.

The total effect of growth plus inflation produces a growth plus inflation factor of 10%. That is, if we really want to be able to say that we are maintaining health spending at a constant level between 1995 and 1997, we need to see a 10% increase.

Specific Health-Oriented Change

A) The aging population

Between 1991 and 1995 the aged population grew by an average of 3.4%. Our adjustment for population growth would capture some of this trend, but we must also account for the increased acuity of care required by elderly people. The vast majority of long term care users are 65 and over. In fact, over 90% of these users are seniors, and half of them are over eighty. The aging of the population is taking place at the same time that the system is shedding beds. The Ontario association of Non-Profit Homes speaks of the effect being to "underbed" the Province, and that its member Homes had to refuse 700 applications in 1996 within Metro Toronto alone because of the lack of bedspace. Metro already has fewer beds per thousand seniors (37.2) than the Ontario average of 44.9 per thousand.

Making things worse, the reduction of the mandatory 2.25 hours of nursing care per day has led to a huge drop in hours of nursing care, from the old standard of 2.25

hours per day to a new low of 2.02.

Simply to restore and maintain the old levels of care would require an additional 3 percent, or $500 million.

B) Hospital Bed-closings and "pushouts"

Rapid bed-closings as a result of the health restructuring exercise acts in a perverse way to place additional costs on long-term care. People are pushed out of hospital faster and faster to cope with the reductions in acute care beds. Home care experts anticipate a province wide costs of some $200 million dollars to put community-based aftercare services in place. This would come from the $500 million fund noted above.

C) Drug costs.

Measures taken by the Mulroney and Chretien governments in Ottawa have created a huge increase in the cost of prescription dugs. The 20-year plus monopoly bestowed on the pharmaceutical industry by Bill C91 has contributed to double digit increases in drug prices. Prescriptions now cost 15 percent of the total health bill. This is as much as we spend on doctors, and twice what we spend on hospitals.

An aggressive campaign by the Ontario government to mandate the use of generic drugs, along the lines of the practice in British Columbia, could produce huge savings. British Columbia saved $21 million in the first ten months of the program. In Ontario, we are convinced that energetic price control measures could save up to 1% off the 10% increase we suggested was needed to maintain real spending.

D) The revision of the 1997–98 budget allocated $218 million which had previously been budgeted for health institutions. It was reassigned to pay for "restructuring." Better it was spent for hospital care instead of hospital shutdowns.

E) Behind all the down loading, privatisation and "profitisation" lies the ideological threat to Medicare itself. As the system is shrunk and pressure on our current institutions becomes intolerable, the drive continues for the establishment of two-tier medicine, with separate facilities and different quality of care, depending on what you can afford to pay.

Summing Up

A budget based on maintaining real spending levels for our health care system will require a three-year catch-up to take into account the combined effects of population growth and inflation. Given the savings from drug price control, this amounts to a 9% increase above the level spent in 1995–96. That means an increase from the 1995–96 base of $17.8 billion to a new level of adequacy of $19.4 billion.

Reversing the recent cuts to hospital care as well as the cuts to mandatory nursing care hours in homes for the aged adds another $500 million, or another 3% on the 1995–96 base.

Measured in per capita terms, the Harris health budget dropped on a real per capita basis from $1,727 per person to $1,584 per person, in 1997 dollars. The 9% increase restores the per capita spending to $1,727. The additional 3% raises it to $1,778.

Table 9.1 Health Budgets, 1995–96 to 1997–98

Programs	1995–96 Official Actual	1996–97 Official Estimate	1997–98 Official Estimate	1997–98 Alternative "A"	1997–98 Alternative "B"
Ministry Administration	131.5	125.2	124.2	130	130
Institutional Health	7,793.3	7,481.4	7,487.4 (*1)	8,495 (*7)	8,550
Health Insurance	5,919.5	5,860.0	6,148.2 (*2)	6,452 (*8)	6,473
Health	685.1	694.9	728.4 (*3)	748	769

Programs	1995-96 Official Actual	1996-97 Official Estimate	1997-98 Official Estimate	1997-98 Alternative "A"	1997-98 Alternative "B"
Population Health & Community Services	1,045.8	1,060.6	982.6 (*4)	1,139	1,173
Long Term Care	2,206.0	2,342.4	2,378.4 (*5)	2,436 (*9)	2,805
Totals		17,812.7	17,564.4	17,849.2	19,400	19,900

Note: The figures in the first three columns are taken from the Ministry of Health Budget Estimates, as submitted to the Ontario Legislative "Standing Committee on Estimates," in June, 1997. The two last columns are approximate Alternative Budgets, for further discussion and input at the local level.

1997–98 Alternative "A" maintains mostly the real levels of the 1995–96 budget, by adding approximately 9% to compensate for population and inflation increases over the three years.

Alternative "B" revives the values of the 1995–96 budget, by adding approximately 3% to the "A" total, mainly in Long Term Care, for reasons described above.

Endnotes

1 Statistics Canada figures show an average yearly growth rate of 3.07% in the Canada-wide senior population. The 1995 figures give 3,558,847 Canadians 65 and over, as compared to a 1991 total of 3,169,965. Statistics Canada projects 4,399,000 by 2006, 6 million by 2021 and 7.5 million by 2031. Among the seniors, the "more elderly" sector, 85 and over, is growing more than twice as fast as the "young seniors," 65 up to 85. Furthermore, women, typically less provided-for financially, have rapidly gained in longevity, going from an average life expectancy of 62 years, two years longer than men, in 1930, to 80 years, 6.4 years longer than men, in 1990. With the positive relation between aging and needed health services, the financial implications of aging should be clear.

2 A 1997 study by the Toronto Office of the Service Employees International Union (SEIU), points to this as an indication of a real crisis in the making, particularly for "the frail elderly." Coming to conclusions parallel to the proposed 3%, or $500 million, add-on in paragraph (3A) above, they go on to say:

As a minimum, we are proposing that the following steps be taken:

HEALTH CARE: THE CRISIS CONTINUES

1. An immediate injection of $144 million dollars into the facility system, to ensure that all facilities are able to maintain the standard of care which was being provided.
2. An immediate 30% increase in long term care beds to accommodate the needs of seniors who are presently waiting for, or unable to access, long term care beds.
3. Restoration of the legislative requirement that all facilities staff a minimum of 2.25 nursing care hours per resident per day, and a concomitant increase in funding, to ensure that staffing at those levels can be maintained. Restoration of the requirement should be tied to the need to acknowledge expressly the "sub-acute" role that long term care facilities are increasingly assuming in the provision of care.
4. An increase in the raw food budget, to ensure that facilities are able to meet the nutritional needs of seniors, and most particularly the needs of seniors who require intravenous feeding.

Looking ahead, the SEIU paper urges:

a) Follow-up on point 2 above with [commitment to] a further 20% increase in beds to provide for the anticipated increase in seniors requiring these services over the next decade.

b) Ongoing study and scrutiny to ensure that funding for long term care facilities continues to keep pace with increasing demands for care in this sector. There is need for an "outcomes" monitoring-based system which measures both "quantity" and "quality" of care issues, including: data collection and analysis, public accessibility, impartial review and auditing on a routine and case-complaint basis, and public disclosure of ownership documents, financial reports, etc.

Chapter Ten

SOCIAL POLICY: WHAT ARE WE WILLING TO DO?

When *Fortune* magazine and the U.N. rank Canada and Canadian cities as the best place to live or do business in, they are paying a great tribute to the strong, adaptive and resilient networks of physical and social infrastructures that we collectively have built. Despite almost two decades of cutbacks and "social thuggery," they still make us distinct.

Canada's high standing in the areas of social cohesion, multicultural diversity, high standard of living and quality of life, liveable urban centres, etc. is the result of a conscious and collective decision to build a strong public framework of physical, cultural and social infrastructures. These public frameworks – medicare, E.I., Canada Assistance Plan, C.P.P., social housing, public works, C.B.C., public education system – are at the centre of Canada's economic successes.

Liberating the so-called entrepreneurial spirit (through deregulation, privatization, contracting out) and cutting public spending has resulted in a country and province where a significant majority of the population harbours serious concerns about both the collective and their own economic and social security.

There is abundant evidence ranging from public surveys, to the World Bank and the World Economic Forum, that income inequality has a significantly negative impact on health outcomes; that employment in secure jobs has a positive impact on the health of workers and their families; that investing in pre-schoolers and kids is the best way to positively influence their personal outcomes and those of their families; that strong, inclusive public programs build a deep sense of social solidarity; that rising inequality does not generate economic success and imposes important economic costs in the form of wasted potential, crime, sickness, and premature death.

Public programmes and spending are critical to promoting and sustaining a strong sense of civic vitality. As the cuts to public spending get deeper and economic and social insecurity heightens it is important to remember that there is a better way. The roots lie in a shared commitment to the values of a re-tooled and citizen-centred social policy.

In less than two years the Harris government has announced $5.5 billion in cuts from it's 1995 budget base, with $3 billion more to come. This is still short of the $10 billion needed to pay for the 30% tax cut and to balance the budget.

The above cuts and others have created a crisis for many of the province's most vulnerable citizens which are beyond the comprehension of the cutters with their nineteenth century views on minimal government and the benefits of the unimpeded market.

In a buoyant labour market these cuts would be serious. However in a stagnant, high-unemployment, low-pay labour market, they are devastating.

The Canadian Council on Social Development (CCSD) recently published an important study, *Left Poor By The Market*, which shows that poor families are significantly worse off in the labour market than 10 years ago.

The study shows (see below) that government attempts to force poor families to be self-reliant by cutting both social programs and financial transfers has resulted in increased poverty. The pervasive presence of an insecure low wage labour market makes self-reliance a bad joke. These figures are from the pre-Harris era, and are undoubtedly much worse in 1997.

Table 10.1 Incidence and Depth of Poverty in Ontario

Incidence (% of working age families)	1984	1994
market poor	17.7	20.3
total poor (after tax & transfers)	11.3	12.9

Depth of Poverty (below poverty line)	1984	1994
market poor	$12,955	$14,749
total poor (after tax & transfer)	$ 9,818	$ 7,998

Unfortunately, social policy in much of the public mind has become synonymous with social assistance. There is both a strong movement to roll back the state in order to remove all obstacles to the workings of the free market and private property (ie. privatization, deregulation, low taxes) and a strong moral agenda of social issues concerning crime, the family, social disorder and dependency.

Social policy generally refers to government policies which try to meet the social needs of the population which the market cannot or will not satisfy, and generally includes income maintenance, housing, health care, education, pensions, law and order, etc.

William Beveridge, the architect of the British Welfare State, saw the aim of the welfare state as the slaying of the five giant evils – Want, Disease, Ignorance, Squalor, and Idleness. The state would do this by providing social policies such as education, pensions, health care, social services, unemployment and sickness benefits, etc. While it would be foolish to deny that significant progress has been made in mitigating these problems, they have clearly not been slain. Indeed in Harris' Ontario their spectre is again haunting Ontarians as poverty and inequality are demonstrably increasing.

The so-called golden age of the post-war welfare state, from 1945–1975, has clearly ended. The general public has been conditioned by two decades of propaganda and lived experience to the arguments of the primacy of deficit reduction and balanced budgets and the inevitable insecurity of work and income.

There is no turning back to the old post-war welfare state: not because of the positive values (equality, social justice, fairness, income security, etc.) it stood for, but because we need a new social arrangement for a changed world.

A new social partnership must deal with profound economic changes and will need a social policy and social security system which deals with this new economic environment. Some current trends are:

- persistent high rates of structural unemployment
- corporate capability to move capital and operations to low wage areas
- end of universality and focus on targeting of social policies
- new family arrangements and structures
- loss of well-paying and secure manufacturing jobs and their replacement with less well paid and insecure contingent (ie. temporary, self-employed, part-time, contract) jobs
- smaller workforce at lower pay supporting benefits required by a growing aging population
- serious impediment to youth (18–25) entry into labour market
- frequent job and career changes

The above factors and others have the potential to lead to both social unrest in general and intergenerational hostility in particular. We could be moving to a 30:30:40 society where 30% are secure with well-paying jobs and are full participants in society, 30% are employed on a contingent and insecure basis and 40% are in an underclass with little prospect of working.

What does social policy look like in such an environment?

Social policy reflects both the values of a country and its image of itself. For example the Swedish welfare state reflects an image of social solidarity and cohesion whereas the American welfare state reflects "rugged individualism," limited government and social mobility. Canada and Ontario, due to popular pressure, have a lukewarm commitment to public medicare – but nevertheless we are clearly moving to the minimalist welfare state model of America.

There are doubts which now go beyond the question of can we afford a welfare state to asking: *should* we afford it? These concerns are rooted in questions about what kind of society we have become and changes in the relationship that should occur between the state and the individual. The real question should be: can we afford not to have generous, user-friendly, inclusive social programs?

Social policy and social programmes are more than social assistance. They are more than income transfers, providing a wide range of services to seniors, employables, unemployables, children and families, the disabled, the poor, students, First Nations, immigrants and visible minorities. They include some but not all of the following: public health, immigrant services, child care, child development, services to women, disabled services, child care, health promotion and health services, employment training programs, social housing, public education, minimum wage and employment standards protection, First Nation services, young offenders.

For the past twenty years, the mainstream media has largely and uncritically accepted the attacks of right-wing think tanks and foundations, corporate lobby groups etc. that the welfare state is out of control; that it is sucking up more and more of society's limited resources; that it is neither sustainable nor desirable; that public spending on social programs severely limits our international competitiveness; that the welfare state tax burden is pushing ordinary families beyond their personal budgets, etc. As a result the "S-word" (spending) has become taboo.

Our alternative budget document – while acknowledging the need to get operating budget deficits under control starts from the premises that:

1) there is no inherent reason why a properly managed and progressively-tax-funded welfare state should be unduly expensive; and

2) the constraints on how much we can tax and spend are less economic than political.

Social policy cannot be designed in a vacuum. It must reflect and interact with the political, economic and value changes of the larger society. A new social policy vision for Ontario would have as a first task the reinstatement of the now-quaint notion of the collective good which is based on those common interests which bind individuals in a collectivity which can still legitimately be called society.

Social policy seeks to remedy both general outcomes that cannot be achieved through the sum of individual activities in the marketplace, and specific setbacks which negatively and adversely affect individuals and their families and which they cannot hope to overcome through their own unassisted efforts. Both problems require systematic interventions defined by agencies to uphold the public good.

The social policy of the 1980s and 1990s was characterized by uneven and declining entitlements. There was access for those empowered through the marketplace and significantly less for those unable to take full advantage of market opportunities.

Whether explicit or not, social policy is rooted in and shaped by abstract ideas about justice. What is fair? What do people have a right to?

Thus we need a new social policy vision which:

1) is coherent and interlocking without imposing excessive uniformity to allow for variations in local practices and outcomes;

2) is based on citizenship rights and meets the full range of a citizen's legitimate aspirations, not merely statistically determined needs;

3) is consistent with policy objectives in other areas (ie. economic, environment, etc.) but is not subservient to them;

4) is efficient in delivery and has built-in audits, inspections and citizen service delivery feedback; and

5) is inclusive and responsive to the different needs and outcomes arising from circumstances of disability, gender, sexual orientation, age, class, language, visible minority status, First Nations status.

The new social policy vision needs to articulate a bottom-line of non-negotiable principles and commitments. What are means and what are ends?

If the name of the game is to take power from the Tories we need to know why and what will be different.

Some non-negotiables could be:

1) fairness and equality;

2) focus on real prevention rather than on curing; and

3) maintain a baseline of security on which people can rely when the market fails them.

The traditional centre-left vision of government has been to manage the economy, to build the welfare state and to ensure a degree of income redistribution. In the new political, economic and value environment of the 1990s should government guarantee perfect security from cradle to grave? Should government assure everyone that they will get a new job if they lose their current one? Should government guarantee the certainty of an adequate pension? Should government guarantee hospital provision of both adequate general and emergency services? Should government guarantee safe streets? Should government guarantee that children achieve some basic educational standards? Should government guarantee a job to everyone who wants one?

The guaranteeing of the above certainties would allow people to get on with their lives, despite the chronic insecurity generated by the marketplace. Needless to say, it is important to stress the positive relationship between a rich social policy and a healthy economy where unemployment is low. Secure, well-paying jobs complemented by pay and employment equity legislation, protective and strong labour standards (minimum wage law), the ability to join a union and bargain collectively, training and educational opportunities, a universal earnings replacement for employment interruptions, and the ability to participate fully in social, political and economic life are the ideal. Only if one of the above is in place can one genuinely claim the best social policy is a job!

Conclusion

An alternative solidarity budget will repudiate the "slash and burn" agenda of the Harris government, and will provide a vision for meeting human needs through progressively tax-financed public services and public investment.

In order to lay a foundation for budgetary decision-making for 1998 it is hoped that an extensive consultation in the fall of 1997 will address some current, critical, and often controversial issues of concern. Ultimately the various sectors – social policy, taxation, fiscal policy, job creation, education, health, and the environment – need to create an alternative vision that is credible and rigorous enough to withstand the inevitable counter-attack.

We would like to suggest that the following topics could be a start for discussion in the consultation process.

1. Restoration or Reform

    Given that the Ontario Alternative Budget would restore

the Harris social assistance funding cuts, and enhance that funding, a question for discussion is;

- should the present social assistance programs based upon the old Canada Assistance Act be restored and maintained?

or

- should major structural reforms be put in place at the same time that funds are reinvested in social assistance?

2. Basic Right to Subsistence

- Is financial need the appropriate criteria for eligibility for income assistance?
- Should income security in Ontario be a single program or are multiple programs required?
- What should distinguish the programs?
- Who should deliver the programs?
- What are the right guidelines for determining adequate benefits, and what is their relation to basic minimum employment standards?

3. The Prospects of Employment for the Unemployed, Underemployed and Unemployable

- Is there an acceptable level of unemployment in Ontario?
- What assumptions are made as to whether unemployment is cyclical ie. temporary or structural?
- Faced with unemployment, what are the responsibilities of the Ontario government and what are the rights and obligations of the individual?
- If individuals have more than made themselves job-ready, but there are no jobs, who is responsible for assisting them to meet their economic, social and cultural needs?

4. Employment Enhancement Activities
    - What are the responsibilities of the Ontario government, the corporate sector, and the individual with respect to training and education?
    - Who is responsible for funding training?
    - What should the relationship be between the provision of income support and participation in employment enhancement programs?
    - What is our position on the use of EI training funds?
5. Social Justice
    - What conception of social justice should inform social policy?
    - How do we insure that social justice principles are reflected in the institutions that deliver social policies?
6. Social Citizenship
    - What is social citizenship?
    - Can social policy undo the exclusionary ills of the social policies of the 1980s and the 1990s?
7. Universalism versus Selectivism
    - Is universalism dead or is it time for a comeback?
    - Should some social policies be universal and others selective?
    - Which ones?
    - Does targeting overcome some problems associated with the above debate?
8. Who delivers social policies?
    - What should be the respective roles of the state, the voluntary sector, the informal sector and the private sector?

Chapter Eleven

Housing: Filling The Void

A Brief History

Since the Second World War, the housing circumstances and conditions of Canadians, including Ontario residents, have improved significantly. Increasingly, we became an urban society – the percentage of people living on farms declined from 27% in 1941 to 6% twenty years later. Older housing units were replaced by higher quality new stock with modern facilities like central heating and indoor plumbing as standard features. Approximately 60% of our housing stock has been built since 1960. While Canada's population doubled in the 25 years following the war, the number of housing dwellings tripled as the average household size dropped by 40%. This was partly due to decreasing family size, but also reflected increases in real wages that resulted in decreased residential overcrowding.

Despite these changes, tenure patterns have remained static. Almost two-thirds (65.5%) of Ontario households are homeowners and one-third (35.5%) are renters – virtually the same as 70 years ago. Profound changes, however, have been and are now taking place in the housing conditions and economic circumstances of owner and renter households. Some of these changes stem from demographic, social and market factors, but the most profound and constant agent shaping the way Canadians house themselves has been government policies and programs.

The Pivotal Role of Government

The federal government established the Canada Mortgage and Housing Corporation (formerly Central Mortgage and Housing Corporation) in 1946 to be responsible for housing supply and rehabilitation programs, undertaking housing research and providing housing information. Since 1954, CMHC has also insured residential mortgages. Ontario, like all other provinces, has a provincial ministry responsible for similar housing functions.

Traditionally, government housing policy has been aimed at ensuring that the private sector could meet the housing needs of the community. A long list of programs have been introduced over the years to stimulate private residential construction. These programs have had two main goals: to encourage as many people as possible to enter into home ownership, and to ensure an adequate supply of rental housing for those unable to afford home ownership. A wide range of direct and indirect public subsidies has been used to achieve these goals. Housing programs have also been viewed by governments as an easy way to boost employment and generate broad economic activity.

In addition to various tax measures and mortgage stabilization initiatives, governments in the recent past provided significant direct subsidies to homeowners and home purchasers. At their height in the early 1980s the cost of the three biggest federal home ownership assistance programs alone surpassed $1 billion per year.

In the private rental sector, massive government subsidies have encouraged the development of new rental stock and, to a lesser extent, the rehabilitation of existing rental housing. By the mid-1970s almost all private rental housing starts in Ontario were subsidized. By 1985, the federal government was spending an estimated $4 to $5 billion per year to subsidize rental production. In addition, the Government of Ontario often supplemented federal programs with provincial funding.

The inability of many low-income households to afford either home-ownership or rental housing supplied by the private sector, despite the public programs and expenditures, led in 1949 to the introduction of Canada's first public housing programs. It was a modest program that on a national basis produced less than 12,000 units by 1964. The programs was greatly expanded in 1964, resulting in a total stock of more than 200,000 units by the mid-1970s – 84,000 of which are located in Ontario. Public housing was targeted exclusively at poor households. Policy makers of the day generally viewed it as a stop-gap form of housing for people temporarily down on their luck, who would then move on to the private rental or ownership sectors after a relatively short stay.

The 1969 Royal Commission Report on Housing and Urban Development heralded a fundamental policy shift away from public housing. Rather than subsidizing the production of government-owned and operated public housing, exclusively targeted at the poor, programs were redirected to community-based non-profit and co-operative housing groups. The new emphasis on the non-governmental sector stressed smaller-scale developments targeted at a mix of low and moderate-income households, who would put down roots in the community. These new programs were largely based on the private sector rental programs of the day, and shared the twin objectives of increasing the supply of rental housing and providing rent supplements to a limited number of needy households. By the mid-1980s, most private rental programs were curtailed, as non-profit and co-op rental housing supply programs became the favoured public policy choice of government.

Constitutionally, housing is a shared federal and provincial responsibility. Prior to 1985 the federal government was the major funder and delivery vehicle for housing programs, some of which were cost-shared with provinces. Since that time the federal government has steadily withdrawn from the field, and has not provided new funding for housing supply programs since 1993.

The government of Ontario, through the Ontario Housing Corporation, is the owner and operator of 84,000 units of public housing. The provincial Ministry of Housing (now the Ministry of Municipal Affairs and Housing) was formed from OHC. The province's role in housing has increased substantially since 1985 when it took over the federal role as the delivery vehicle and funding body for all housing supply programs. During the late 1980s and early 1990s Ontario introduced several large-scale unilaterally-funded non-profit housing supply programs.

Ontario's Housing System

Most of our residential housing – an astounding 93.3% – is privately owned. The remainder is collectively owned by governments, and a variety of non-profit, co-operative or charitable community-based organizations. Private sector firms do all the building, supply the materials and dominate the real estate development and mortgage lending sectors.

The residential development and construction sector is for the most part comprised of small firms that each produce a relatively small volume of ownership housing. A few large firms grew out of some of these smaller firms during the apartment construction boom of the 1950s and 1960s. Many of the larger players moved into the condominium market following the introduction of condominium tenure in the mid-1960s, as well as diversifying into industrial, retail and commercial development. While many of these large firms once held substantial portfolios of private rental housing, only a few remain in a sector now dominated by companies with little or no direct involvement in new home development.

The Last Ten Years – A Contrast of Decades

The 1990s have been a time of significant change for many sectors in the Ontario economy. Some of the most radical changes, in terms of their magnitude, have occurred in housing. During the late 1980s Ontario's strong economy and rapid growth fuelled a major housing boom. Between 1986 and 1989, the average purchase price of a home in Ontario jumped by 71% and shot up by a whopping 98% in the Toronto area. The construction industry experienced shortages of materials and labour, as annual housing starts during the same period averaged nearly 100,000 units.

Similarly, growth-related pressures also rocked the rental market. Vacancy rates in the province remained below 1% throughout the late 1980s, and hovered near zero in Metro Toronto. The shortage of rental housing put considerable upward pressure on rents and created a black market in which bribes or "key money" were often demanded for good quality, well-located apartments. Trapped in renting by high home prices, consumer affordability for renters was further eroded by property speculation.

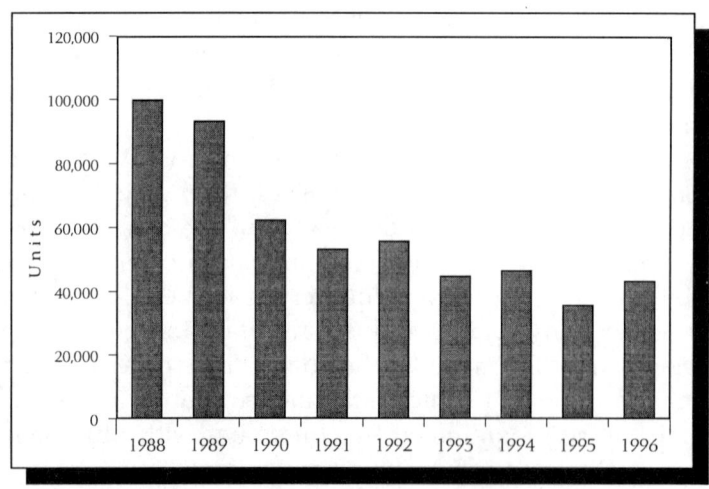

Figure 11.1 Housing Starts in Ontario, 1988–96

Source: Canada Mortgage and Housing Corporation. Prepared by the Co-operative Housing Federation of Canada.

In contrast, the housing market of the 1990s has been typified by decreases in ownership prices and sluggish residential construction activity. Housing starts for the first half of the

1990s declined by 45% compared to levels of the late 1980s. Average home prices in Ontario fell 13% by 1994 from their 1989 peak. Toronto saw a 24% price drop over the same period. People who purchased at the height of the market experienced a loss in equity. However, all mortgage payers benefited from lower mortgage rates that greatly reduced monthly carrying costs. Lower prices coupled with the lowest mortgage interest rates in decades combined to dramatically improve the prospects for first-time home buyers.

Figure 11.2 Toronto CMA Vacancy Rates, Private Apartments – Three Units and Over

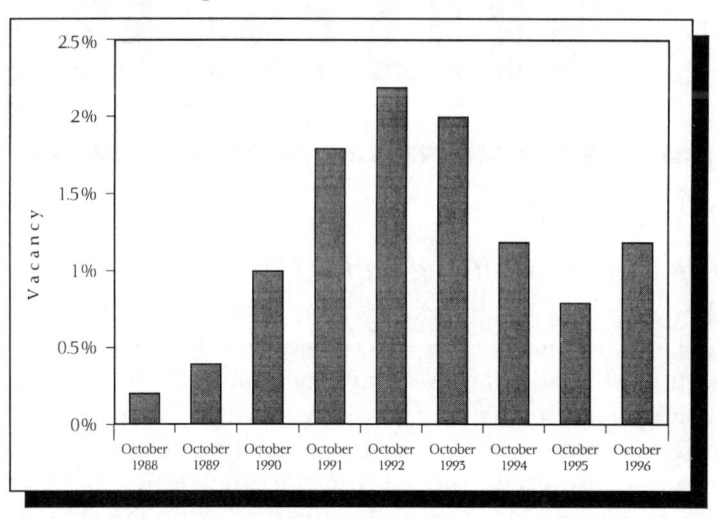

Source: Canada Mortgage and Housing Corporation. Prepared by the Co-operative Housing Federation of Canada.

For renters, the 1990s brought a mixed blessing. Unlike ownership prices, rents continued to rise – increasing by 13.6% between 1990 and 1995. Indeed, the cost of renting in the first half of the decade actually out-paced inflation. On the bright side, Ontario's vacancy rate more than doubled, and Toronto's rate briefly crested over 2% before falling back below 1%. This resulted in more choice for tenant households, and helped to somewhat dampen rent increases.

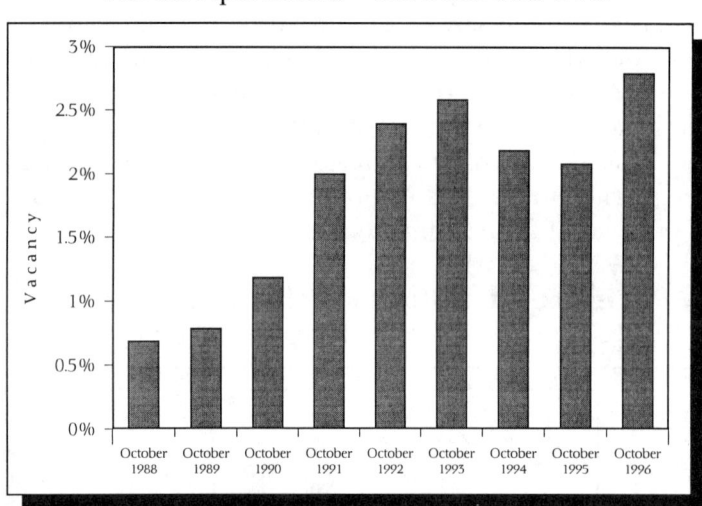

Figure 11.3 Ontario CMA Vacancy Rates, Private Apartments – Six Units and Over

Source: Canada Mortgage and Housing Corporation. Prepared by the Co-operative Housing Federation of Canada.

The Current Housing Policy Context

The federal government has all but abandoned the housing field. Its current activities are confined to funding an extremely modest residential housing rehabilitation program, supporting home ownership through the RRSP down-payment program, and running the government-backed mortgage insurance program. Indeed, the once-powerful CMHC has had its corporate mandate trimmed to supplying housing research and information, developing international trade opportunities, and providing mortgage insurance.

As part of completing the federal withdrawal from programs that actively address the housing needs of Canadians, the federal government is currently attempting to formally devolve its existing role in social housing to provincial and territorial governments. On a bilateral basis the federal government has already negotiated social housing transfer agreements with three provinces and one territory. Active negotiations are underway with the remaining provincial and territorial governments. Under the deals signed to date, the federal government hands over the general responsibility for housing along with the administration of social housing created through previous federal or cost shared programs and the $1.9 billion in federal funding currently earmarked for such programs.

While the federal government claims devolution is simply about clarifying roles and eliminating duplication, the move fits nicely with their current fiscal objectives. By the end of the term of the federal transfer agreements with provincial and territorial governments, federal spending on social housing will have been totally eliminated.

Premier Mike Harris and members of his government have often repeated that their guiding housing objective is to "get government out of the housing business, and let the private sector do the job." In their view the job of government is to create the environment in which the private sector can meet *all* the housing requirements of the people of the province. They believe the government's role should be reduced as much as possible, and confined to removing market impediments and providing minimal income supports to the truly needy so they can access housing in the private market.

Almost all non-profit and co-op housing developments were cancelled soon after the current government took office in June 1995. At the time the government insisted that the private sector would fill the void, thus offsetting the loss of some 17,000 new non-profit and co-operative dwellings. To that end, various environmental, planning and consumer protections have been eliminated or weakened. The rental housing market is being re-regulated to allow for the demolition and conversion of existing rental housing, while other tenant protections and rights, such as rent controls, are being reduced or eliminated.

More recently, the province announced that it will completely devolve its role in housing to the municipalities. The provincial plan calls for municipal governments to take on the funding and administration of the 84,000 units of public housing, as well as the 190,000 units of community-based non-profit and co-operative housing. Municipalities have uniformly and strenuously opposed the idea that they take on the responsibility for housing and pay for housing program through their property tax revenue. Housing providers and advocates have also opposed the province's plan, fearing that the capacity of the municipal property tax base will be unable to support the cost of housing and the other social programs the province is down loading, while continuing to cope with the existing municipal service envelope.

Current Housing Outlook

Most housing transactions are financed through the use of mortgages. The cost of capital financing is almost always the largest single cost associated with the production of rental housing or the purchase of ownership housing. Currently, mortgage interest rates are at their lowest point in more than thirty years. This has allowed many higher income renters to buy their first home, and has significantly reduced the carrying cost for homeowners and rental investors alike. It has also sparked a moderate resurgence in the residential construction sector. Unlike the 1980s when higher priced move-up and luxury dwellings were popular, the current market is more price sensitive as consumers lack of confidence – both in terms of property value appreciation and job security. Consequently, the resale market is seeing more activity at the low end; the new homes tend to be smaller and more modest. The increase in construction activity, however, is almost exclusively limited to the ownership stock.

The outlook in the rental sector is bleak, particularly for consumers. Non-profit and co-op housing, which accounted for the vast majority of the rental housing starts in the last fifteen years, have been curtailed with the cancellation of programs at the federal and provincial levels. All indications are that renters are facing a very difficult era in future years, as three major issues confront tenants and policy makers: shortage of new supply; deterioration of the existing stock; and the growing problem of affordability.

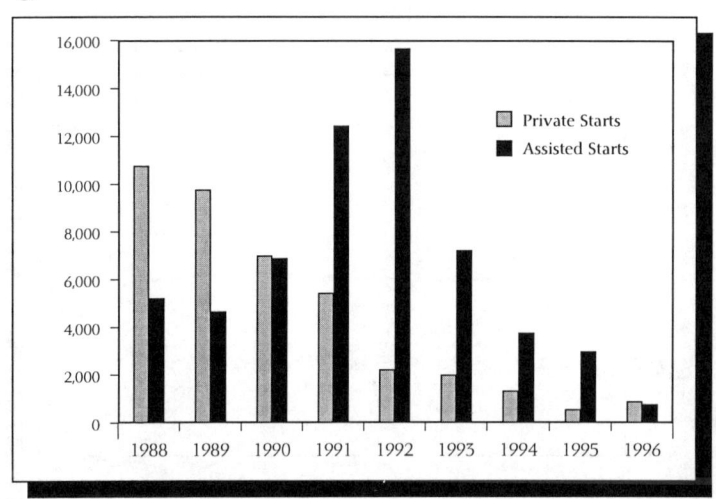

Figure 11.4 Private and Assisted Rental Starts in Ontario

Source: Canada Mortgage and Housing Corporation. Prepared by the Co-operative Housing Federation of Canada.

(i) New Supply

Ontario is entering completely uncharted territory – a policy and program vacuum – in terms of rental housing supply. For more than half a decade the supply of rental housing has been driven by government programs and tax policy. Despite the Harris government's predictions and efforts, there is no indication that the private sector has or will respond to the need for more new rental housing. This is the case despite the fact that low interest rates have created the most favourable market conditions for rental investment in decades, and the government is making every regulatory change the development industry has demanded. In Toronto, Canada's largest city, where CMHC estimates a need for between 5,000 and 6,000 new rental units per year, there were only 37 starts in 1996 – and even they were life-lease units aimed at older empty-nest homeowners.

As is the case in all other industrialized countries, very little (if any) rental housing is produced by the private sector without government assistance. The reason for this is that the

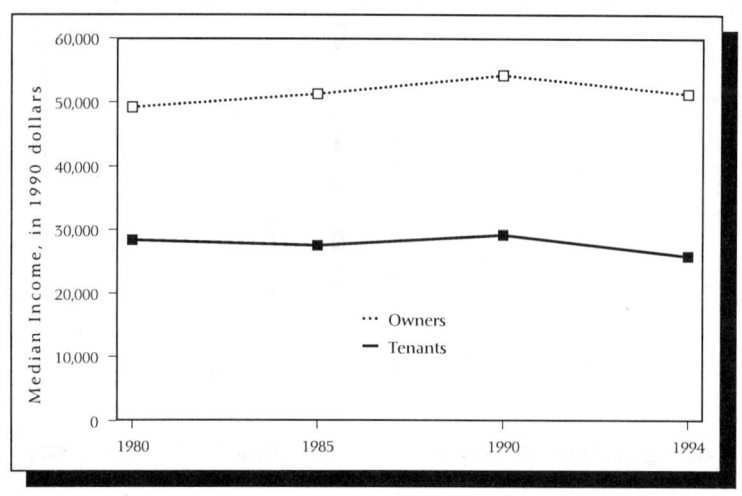

Figure 11.5 Median Incomes of Renters and Owners, 1980–94

Source: 1981, 1986 and 1991 Census & Household Income, Facilities & Equipment Survey, 1995, Statistics Canada & Lapointe Consulting. Prepared by the Co-operative Housing Federation of Canada.

housing market very effectively segregates people on the basis of whether or not they can afford to pay the economic cost of their shelter. Compared to renting, Canadians almost universally prefer the benefits of home ownership. As a result, those who can afford to buy a home almost always do, often making great sacrifices to do so. The rental market is overwhelmingly comprised of people who can't afford home ownership. In some cases this is attributable to chronically low incomes; in others it is because they are too young to have yet reached their peak income earning potential, or have aged beyond those peak earning years. In terms of cost, there is no real difference between the production cost of an entry-level ownership housing unit and a rental housing unit. Both products conform to the same requirements, and make use of the same materials and labour. The prospective builder of a new rental project cannot successfully compete in the market place directly against the builder of modest ownership housing. Traditionally, government rental supply programs – whether directed at the private sector or the non-profit sector – have all sought to bridge the gap between the cost of production and what renters can reasonably afford.

Figure 11.2 Age Distribution of Owner and Renter Households in Ontario

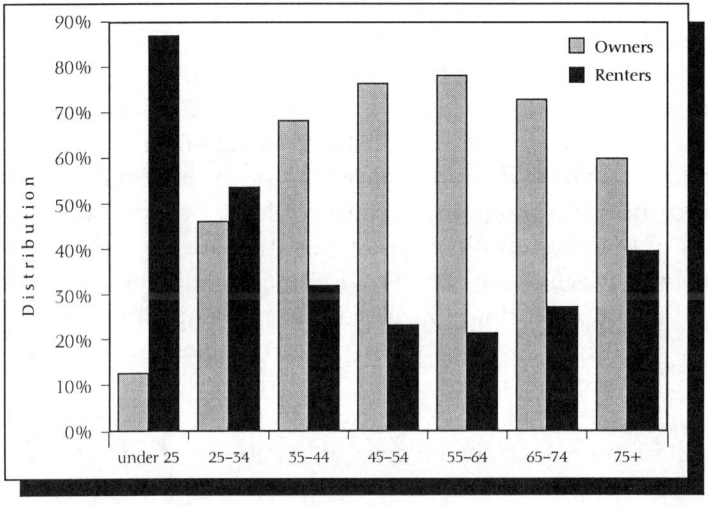

Source: 1991 Census, Statistics Canada. Prepared by the Co-operative Housing Federation of Canada.

Three factors have spared Ontario, for the time being, from a drastic shortage of rental housing:

- non-profit and co-op projects that were already in the production pipeline, and were not cancelled by the Harris government, continued to deliver completed new units until recently;
- low interest rates have enabled higher income renters to move into the home ownership market, easing pressure on the rental market; and
- the recession and government cuts have forced some households to change their living arrangements – doubling up, young adults moving back home or simply not leaving.

All of these factors, however, are temporary and the pent-up demand will not simply go away.

Ontario is faced with a combination of a growing population and no new rental supply on the horizon. As interest rates rise, the unavoidable shortage of rental housing will soon create a drag on economic growth, similar to that which occurred in the late 1980s. And low-income households will increasingly find it difficult to compete in a tight market.

To exacerbate further an already grim outlook, the province's plan to devolve the responsibility for housing to municipalities threatens to institutionalize the rental housing shortage. No other jurisdiction in the industrialized world funds housing programs exclusively from property taxes. The cost of housing people who can't afford housing that the market produces is significant. Provincial and federal governments have far more taxing power than do municipalities which are almost completely reliant on property taxes. In light of the integral income maintenance and redistributive nature of housing programs, these costs are also most appropriately dealt with through the income taxing ability of senior levels of government.

(ii) Existing Supply

The existing supply of rental housing continues to age and deteriorate – 54% of all rental buildings are more than 25 years old. More than 7% of Ontario's rental stock is officially classed by Statistics Canada as being in need of major repair and another 19% is in need of minor repair. The economics of the rental market do not encourage proper maintenance and timely remedial work. To ensure the existing stock remains viable, and does not unnecessarily add to the need for new supply, steps will be required to deal with this growing problem.

(iii) Housing Affordability

There is a growing gap between the incomes of owners and renters – renters are increasingly typified by their low incomes, and the fact that they spend a much greater share of their income on the cost of housing. Owner incomes are now almost double those of renters. More than ½ million tenant households in Ontario pay more than 30% of their income on rent and nearly half of those pay more than 50% of their income on rent. In 1988, the percentage of private sector tenants paying more than 30% of their income on rent was 25.9%; by 1995 that had increased to 38.2%, while those paying more than 50% increased from 10.1% to 15.8% over the same period.

The biggest housing program in Ontario continues to be the social assistance system and its shelter allowances. Cuts to social assistance have hurt the 29% of Ontario renters who rely on benefits to help pay the rent. While the Harris government's Common Sense Revolution promised to end the two-year waiting list for affordable housing, two years after being elected the waiting lists have continued to grow. In Toronto alone, the waiting list for public housing stands at 36,000 households.

What are the Options?

In attempting to address the rental housing needs of Canadians, governments have used public funding to subsidize three groups to develop and operate rental housing; the private sector, the public sector, and the non-profit/co-op sectors. Each approach has its benefits and drawbacks.

Public housing was designed to house people who could not afford rental housing in the private market. Government halted the expansion of public housing in the late 1960s following a Royal Commission Report that identified 'ghettoisation' of poor people and lack of community support as major drawbacks. More recently, disrepair and bad management have been identified as problems.

Private sector subsidies both for supply and income support have been used extensively since the Second World War. They have been based on direct subsidies and tax breaks. When these programs ran alongside non-profit/co-op programs they were generally deemed to be more costly, or to provide fewer benefits to lower income households.

Non-profit/co-op housing has been the favoured approach for the past twenty years because of its community-based nature and its relative cost effectiveness. In the context of mounting public debt it has been criticized as being too costly and not serving all of those in need.

The current approach is not to have publicly-funded housing programs at all. As a result, these is virtually no new production of rental housing. But the down side of inaction is that more households get pushed to the margins, we see a growth in homelessness and a greater reliance on other social and community services like policing and food banks. Poor housing conditions also have costs stemming from people being unable to participate in normal community life – low levels of academic achievement for children, difficulty holding or finding employment for adults, and community instability.

A Three-Point Rental Housing Program Model

As a starting point for discussion and consultation, the following three-point non-profit/co-op housing model is presented along with the associated costs and inputs. This model is not an attempt to fashion a comprehensive housing policy – since that would, at a minimum, also require that legislative and other issues be addressed. Rather, it is an attempt to look exclusively at housing from a budgetary and program perspective by addressing the three key elements in the housing equation:

- A rental housing supply program that targets the production of 3,000 to 5,000 new units annually.
- A rental housing stabilization and rehabilitation program aimed at tenants being able to secure and rehabilitate approximately 5,000 existing units per year.
- A rent supplement program that will provide up to 5,000 new rent-geared-to-income subsidies annually to low-income households.

1. New supply initiative

This would be a new program not based on any previous program. It would operate on an up-front capital loan system, with no ongoing cost to government other than the separate rent supplement program. Eligible non-profit and co-operative sponsors, competing in different streams, would be allowed interest-free loans of up to 40% of initial capital cost in order to build new developments that would be viable at prevailing market rents.

The goal would be to create a program that relied heavily on a real partnership with community sponsors, incentives rather than regulation to drive cost effectiveness, and predetermined exposure for government. This would dramatically minimize the need for government oversight and administration and reduce costs compared to earlier programs.

Costs:

- year one – $120 million for interest-free repayable loans (3,000 units)
- year two – $160 million for interest-free repayable loans (4,000 units)
- year three – $120 million for interest-free repayable loans (5,000 units)

    Note: The full amount of the interest-free loan has been booked as if it is expensed in total at the outset. Repayment would begin once the first mortgage is retired. As a result no input for loan repayment has been included.

Inputs (not including repayment):

- year one – 6,600 person years of employment, $45 million in provincial taxes
- year two – 8,800 person years of employment, $60 million in provincial taxes
- year three – 11,000 person years of employment, $75 million in provincial taxes

Note: both inputs and costs for new supply would be felt during the year(s) of construction. There is a natural planning and pre-development lag period between the announcement of such initiatives and when their construction impact is felt.

2. Rental stabilization and rehabilitation initiative

Under this initiative, existing tenants would be eligible to form non-profit co-operatives for the purpose of attempting to organize the acquisition of the rental housing complexes in which they live. The program would operate on the same principles of real partnership with community sponsors, incentives rather than regulation to drive cost effectiveness and pre-determined exposure for government that lie behind the supply initiative.

Successful tenant group partners would be able to access loan guarantees for up to 25% of the purchase price. The project would need to be financially viable based on the existing or post-acquisition rents – no ongoing funding. In addition, successful groups would be eligible to access a pool of special rehabilitation funds that would operate on the same basis as the federal residential rehabilitation program – the funds appear as a loan on title and sponsors earn forgiveness over a ten year period. In order to avoid the 'basket case' problem, only properties with significant life remaining in the basic components and where the repairs can be done without tenant dislocation would be accepted. The maximum rehab loan would $10,000 per unit.

Cost:

- Acquisition loan pool – $75 million annually; direct cost would only be incurred in cases of default. The rehabilitation component would involve a one-time only cost of $50 million for each year of the program.

Inputs:

- Every 5,000 units would generate 2,200 person years of employment, plus some un-calculated tax revenue.

Note: The lag referred to above for new supply is greatly reduced for acquisition and rehabilitation. Often all or a good part of these impacts can be felt in the same year as the initiative is announced.

3. Rent supplement initiative

This would be a 'stacking' program that would be designed to run parallel to the two previous initiatives. It would allow low income and special needs households to access and remain secure within the new or acquired housing. The maximum rent supplement level would be 60% for the new supply component and 40% for the acquisition component. The difference reflects the fact that existing properties tend to have lower rents than new units and thus can house a similar income profile with fewer rent supplements. Again, in contrast to the existing provincial program, simplicity would be the goal and would result in little or no ongoing government overhead cost.

Cost: $25 million for each 5,000 rent supplement units. However, unlike the previous two components, rent supplement program costs are long-term annual commitments.

Offset: Many of the households which would be eligible for rent supplement would already be receiving social assistance. The offset needs to be determined.

Questions for consultation

Should the government of Ontario take steps to ensure that all Ontario residents, regardless of their income, have access to decent, affordable housing?

Should public funds be used to meet the housing needs of Ontario households?

If so, what kind of vehicle should be used to address the need of Ontarians for more new rental housing: government-owned and managed public housing, privately-owned and managed rental housing, or community-owned non-profit and co-op housing? Or something else?

What approach should be used to ensure that our existing rental housing is well maintained and that repairs are done to ensure a reasonably long physical life?

How can we best ensure that low income households are able to pay for their rent and still put food on the table?

Should all programs that help people pay the rent be handled by one government ministry?

What level of funding should Ontario's provincial budget target for housing – 1%, 10%, 25%?

Should the province keep its programs for first-time homeowners, like the discount on the Land Transfer Tax and the Ontario Homeownership Savings Plan?

What other housing measures would you propose?

Chapter Twelve

LOCAL GOVERNMENT AND PUBLIC SERVICES IN ONTARIO: DISENTANGLEMENT OR DISCOMBOBULATION?

Municipalities and school boards deliver most of the services that are most visible to Ontarians in their day-to-day lives. In public opinion surveys, local government scores higher than the provincial and federal governments in both general satisfaction and perceived "value for money."

The importance of local government is more than matter of perception. Total program spending under provincial jurisdiction – provincial and local government programs combined – amounts to approximately $72 billion in 1994. Over $32 billion of that total – nearly 45% – was delivered by local governments.

That figure rises to over 60% when medicare is removed from the provincial total.

Local government also has an important place in Ontario's democratic traditions. Local government preceded responsible government at the provincial level in Ontario by over half a century, with the establishment of the first school boards just after the turn of the 19th century.

Not surprisingly, then, local governments have been central to every stage of the wave of progressive reform in public services in Ontario that began in the early 1960s. Public services could not have been expanded without the active engagement of local governments.

By the same token, it would have been impossible to contemplate a major reduction in the size of the public sector in Ontario without the active engagement of local governments. Thus the attack on local government plays a crucial role in the Harris government's strategy to downsize public services.

Local Government and the Common Sense Revolution

While school boards, and particularly their trustees and administrators, were singled out for special attack in the Conservatives' pre-election "bible," the Common Sense Revolution (CSR), there was little said about other aspects of the relationship between the provincial and local governments.

If anything, the CSR went out of its way to give the impression that a Harris government would have a particularly high regard for local governments as institutions. A Harris government was to be a decentralizing government which would, at the same time, avoid the sin of "downloading" of which it accused both the NDP and Liberal governments before it.

In the first two rounds of cuts, the government evidently assumed that it could count on local governments to cut the size of the public sector simply by cutting back on its funding transfers to local governments. In particular, it was assumed either that local governments would enthusiastically embrace the neo-conservative revolution, or that local political leaders would be so impressed by the Harris mandate that they would acquiesce in the face of the overwhelming "winds of change."

Things did not work out exactly as planned. Far from reacting with enthusiasm to the opportunity to endorse welfare cuts, municipalities – particularly urban municipalities – became focal points for opposition to the Harris agenda.

School boards were even less "cooperative." The Harris promise not to touch classroom spending notwithstanding, boards responded to the $400 million cut in funding announced in 1995 by making high-profile cuts in programming – canceling junior kindergarten, increasing class sizes and laying off teachers, or defying the government and increasing local property taxes in order to maintain public services.

The Harris Government and "Disentanglement"

By the spring of 1996, both the economics and the politics of the Common Sense Revolution were in jeopardy. It was clear that the spending cuts in the CSR would fall at least $3 billion short of what would be needed to cover the combined cost of the tax cut and balancing the budget. Having promised to maintain health care spending, the government was faced with the reality that the additional cuts would have to come primarily from education and services delivered by municipal governments.

That posed the political problem. Based on the experience of the first two rounds of cuts, school boards and municipalities could not be relied upon as agents of the CSR. For the Harris Conservatives, "disentanglement" emerged as the mechanism the government needed to lever the expenditure cuts they needed to pay for their tax cut while at the same time establishing the means to manage the political reaction to the cuts.

In the past 12 years, there have been six major reviews of provincial and municipal responsibilities: the Provincial-Municipal Social Services Review; the Hopcroft Report; the so-called "disentanglement" exercise of the previous government; the Property Tax Working Group of the Ontario Fair Tax Commission; the Fair Tax Commission itself; and the Crombie "Who Does What?" panel. These exercises were initiated by four different governments representing three political parties. They approached the issue of appropriate local and provincial responsibilities from a number of different perspectives: governance, efficiency, accountability, tax fairness. And they all came to the same conclusion: local governments should be primarily responsible for the funding of local "hard" services; the provincial government should be primarily responsible for the funding of "people" services.

A closer look at the conclusions of these studies, however, reveals a number of factors that make their implementation much more complicated than the apparent simplicity of the term would suggest. First, a reform that followed the logic to the letter would result in a substantial transfer of financial responsibility from local governments to the provincial government. The programs related to income redistribution or services to people whose funding would shift to the provincial government were far larger than the programs related to "hard" services that would be assumed by municipal governments. These reviews dealt with this problem in a number of different ways. In the reviews up to and including the "disentanglement" exercise of the previous government, education was not included in the scope of the study. The Fair Tax Commission made the shift of financial responsibility from the local property tax to provincial revenue sources an explicit and central part of its package of recommendations. The Crombie "Who does what?" panel took pains to separate education funding from the general logical structure of its report.

Second, none of these reviews actually delivered the "disentanglement" that they promised. Even where the direction suggested by the logic was clear, they generally recommended the continuation, often in a different form, of the partnerships that defined the "entanglements" they claimed to be addressing. Municipalities would continue to share in the administration of social services; the provincial government would continue to have an interest in local roads and sewer and water systems. There would continue to be a strong local component to school administration and financing.

Third, the logic itself often did not lead to clear conclusions. In areas like policing and public transit, services for people with disabilities, and child care, strong cases could be made for both local and provincial funding and administration. For example, the apparently obvious suggestion that transit be a local responsibility would leave Ontario as virtually the only jurisdiction in the world in which public transit was not subsidized from the revenues of a national or state government.

Fourth, the impact of the suggested changes varied widely from service to service and from local government to local government. Because the "soft" services to be assumed by the provincial government tended to be "urban" services while "hard" services made up a disproportionate share of the budgets of rural municipalities, and because the provincial grants system in general tended to be biased in favour of rural and northern municipalities, "disentanglement" tended to reduce funding obligations for urban municipalities and increase them for rural and northern municipalities.

Finally, because local responsibility tended to produce different standards of service from one community to another, depending on local politics, financial resources and needs, provincializing local "soft" services raised difficult questions about the level of service to be provided in the new structure. "Leveling up" would be extremely expensive; and "leveling down" would cause hardship to the individuals affected.

From Disentanglement to Discombobulation: The Harris Downloading Scheme

None of these features of "disentanglement" was at all attractive to the Harris Conservatives. The objective of the exercise was to reduce provincial costs, not increase them. Getting control of education was the key to the whole puzzle for them, but applying the same logic to municipal services would result in transfers of billions of dollars in fiscal responsibility to the province. To the most anti-urban government in Ontario since World War II, the idea that urban areas in general would gain from disentanglement at the expense of rural areas was abhorrent. And the last thing the government wanted to get into was a debate about whether province-wide standards for public services should match the pre-reform standards in urban areas like Toronto, Ottawa, Hamilton and Sudbury.

Thus, when the provincial government announced its response to the "Who does what?" panel report, all that was left of the logic of disentanglement was the word – with its politically attractive suggestion that duplication and waste would be eliminated, and the image of an electrician's nightmare that formed the foundation for a blizzard of taxpayer-funded advocacy advertising.

In the key area of social services, the government moved in the opposite direction from that recommended by every one of the studies and reviews. Rather than reducing local government's responsibility for social services, the plan would have increased them. Services that had been entirely provincially funded in the past (like long-term care for the elderly) were to be pushed down onto municipal governments and their property taxpayers. Programs like housing, that had never even been considered as candidates for reform in the past, were also to be dumped on local governments. The local role in education funding and governance was to be wiped out, setting Ontario's children up to be the cash cow for an income tax cut that average Ontarians will barely notice.

When a storm of protest arose, the Government still refused to open up the process. It went behind closed doors with the Association of Municipalities of Ontario, put a gun to AMO's head, and came up with a different scheme. Harris backed away from the most unpopular of the downloads – welfare and long-term care. Instead of being responsible for 50% of welfare, municipalities would be responsible for 20%. And the long-term care download was abandoned entirely. But in return, the government *broadened* the welfare download to include family benefits. Most important, Harris has moved the provincial government directly into the residential property tax field, declaring its intention to raise $2.5 billion for education from a provincial residential property tax. And the government's position on housing didn't change, despite widespread opposition and the threat of a legal challenge from the federal government.

The new scheme pacified some of the opposition, but there is still a download of at least $800 million; control of education is still a central piece of the puzzle; and the Provincial invasion of the previously-local property tax base is broadened to include the residential as well as the commercial and industrial tax base.

Market value reassessment is an important component of the government's strategy. The uniform commercial and industrial tax for education that is central to the shift of control over education to Queen's Park cannot take place without market value assessment. Half the residential taxpayers in Ontario will see tax increases – many of them substantial – from reassessment alone. The abolition of the business tax will shift hundreds of millions more from banks and big business onto residential and small business taxpayers. And all of this change – all of this disruption – is driven by the provincial takeover of education.

The Final Piece of the Puzzle: Megacity

The megacity legislation, amalgamating all the local governments of Metro Toronto into a single city, on its face makes no sense in the Harris-Tory view of the world. It creates bigger government. It eliminates the level of government "closest to the people." It centralizes the administration of public services. In its implementation, the government has clearly and unequivocally rejected the overwhelming results of a referendum conducted under new rules that the Harris government itself created. The megacity only makes sense when it is understood for its role in paying for Mike Harris' income tax cut.

The megacity's creation is an implicit acknowledgment by the Harris government of the savagery of the download of costs onto Metro Toronto. And by eliminating the local level of government in Metro, Harris clearly hoped to silence local voices in opposition to his other policies.

The Harris scheme does not reduce provincial/local entanglement. In fact, it increases it. The scheme does not increase accountability and transparency – it reduces it. Billions of dollars have been allocated to vaguely-defined emergency and transition funds that the government will be free to distribute in accordance with its political needs, rather than any defined criteria to which it might be held accountable.

What the Harris Scheme will Do

1. *The Harris Conservatives' scheme will shift a minimum of $819 billion in provincial costs off the provincial balance sheet and down to municipalities.*

In its public statements about its provincial/local government finance package, the government has claimed consistently that every dollar of additional funding responsibility transferred to municipal governments is balanced by additional financial responsibility assumed by the provincial government. That is not true. It is not true for the municipal sector as a whole. And it is emphatically not true for individual municipalities.

Even the numbers provided by the government itself make it clear that when the dust settles, the provincial government's spending will have dropped by $666 million and municipal obligations, funded from property taxes, will have increased by the same amount.

Table 12.1 Summary of Provincial/Local Government Financial Changes of Harris Government

Program Area	Original Plan $ million	Revised Plan $ million
Additional provincial responsibilities		
Replace residential portion of education property tax	5,400	2,500
Less vacant commercial and industrial counted in above	(700)	(150)*
Community reinvestment fund	1,000	500

Program Area	Original Plan $ million	Revised Plan $ million
Less cancellation of municipal unconditional grant program	(666)	(666)
Responsibilities shifted from province to municipalities		
Community police financing	(180)	(162)
Farm tax rebate	(165)	(170)
Property assessment services	(120)	(119)
Social housing	(890)	(905)
Municipal transit and GO transit	(165)	(354)
Libraries	(20)	(15)
Public health	(225)	(225)
Ambulance services	(200)	(200)
Homes for special care	(25)	–
Ferry services and municipal airports	(15)	(15)
Fire and sewer and water inspections	(10)	(10)
Provincial highways transfer	(75)	
Sewer and water support	(100)	
Housing capital cost	(70)	
Children's Aid/Women's Shelters	75	
Shared Funding		
Social assistance	(2,665)	(883)
Child care	(270)	(65)
Long-term health care	(1,150)	–
Tax / fee transfers		
Gross receipts to province	(100)	(90)
Provincial offenses revenues to municipalities	65	65
Additional transition	70	
Net Amount	**(1,346)**	**(819)**[†]

[*] Government estimates that vacant C & I accounts for $400 million of total residential taxes for education; half of that amount would be $200 million; estimate based on available data is a total of $700 million; half of that amount would be $150 million higher than government estimate.

† Additional transition assistance counted in provincial figures as permanent funding; if it were considered temporary, total download would be $879 million.

Note: All data are Government estimates; these estimates are controversial, with critics claiming that costs of additional municipal responsibilities are understated and additional provincial responsibilities overstated.

Table 12.1 contains information provided by the government. It includes the information provided by the government at the time of the announcement of its "Who does what?" response, as well as additional information obtained later.

Neither the download as originally announced, or the revised deal "negotiated" with AMO counted the cancellation of the Municipal Unconditional Grants program – a $666 million item – or the full costs to municipalities of assuming additional responsibilities for provincial highways, sewer and water funding and housing maintenance.

The accounting originally released by the government did not include another major item that fundamentally affects the allocation of obligations between the levels of government. The table showed a credit to the provincial government for additional education tax "room" that would become available to municipalities when the province assumed the share of education costs currently paid from the residential property tax. The figure included in the table was the amount reported as education taxes levied at the residential tax rate. But this figure includes taxes raised for education purposes from vacant commercial and industrial properties, which are taxed at the residential tax rate. Because this revenue follows the education portion of commercial and industrial taxation as an offset to provincial education spending, the balance sheet understated the provincial gain from the downloading scheme by the amount of education tax collected from vacant commercial and industrial properties.

In the revised proposal, the government acknowledged the mistake it had made in its initial proposal, but underestimated the amount involved. According to the government, taxes on vacant commercial and industrial property for education purposes amount to $400 million per year. Estimates for 1993, however, showed a total of approximately $700 million. With the province now levying its own education tax on residential property at half the previous rate, this means that the understatement of provincial gain drops to $150 million (half the difference between $700 million and $400 million). Far from being balanced, on an on-going basis the scheme results in a net gain of over $800 million at the expense of municipalities and their property taxpayers.

Because municipalities and school boards differ in their expenditure patterns and their dependency on provincial grants, the impact of these changes varies widely across the province. For example, Metropolitan Toronto estimates that the scheme will cost Metro $347 million, without taking into account Metro's share of the education tax on vacant commercial and industrial property (estimated to be about $60 million). Ottawa–Carleton estimates that the scheme will force costs up by $86.6 million; Hamilton–Wentworth, $80 million.

While Metro, Ottawa and Hamilton are the biggest victims of the scheme in absolute terms, other communities will be even harder-hit in relative terms. Sudbury will lose $73.6 million. Thunder Bay will lose $37.7 million; Durham $34.5 million; Niagara $34.3 million. The costs of the Harris scheme will inevitably be significant in many other areas of the province as well.

2. *The scheme will give the government the levers it needs to reduce Ontario's commitment to public education and reap the fiscal benefits.*

The provincial government currently funds only about 35% of the cost of elementary and secondary education in the province, even when the provincial contribution to the teachers' pension fund is included. This compares with the average for other provinces of about 80%. This has two important implications for the Harris downloading scheme.

First, a 35% share of funding on average across the province does not provide enough leverage either to force school boards to cut services as a response to cuts in provincial grants, or to influence the areas in which spending cuts were made. That fact is obvious when you look at the responses of school boards to the $400 million provincial funding cut announced in the fall of 1995. Most school boards either raised taxes, cut highly-visible services, or increased class sizes overall — all contrary to the Harris government's stated intention of targeting non-classroom expenses.

Second, to the extent that changes imposed by the provincial government actually result in reduced spending on education, only 40% of the resulting savings would accrue to the provincial government. Fully 60% would accrue to school boards and their property taxpayers. From the perspective of the provincial government, this presents the unattractive proposition of having to pay the political price for imposing the cuts, but being unable to recoup more than 40% of the resulting savings.

It has been clear right from the beginning that the Harris Conservatives really have no goals of their own for education reform. Their sole interest is in using the education system as a cash cow from which to fund part of their income tax cut. And that, in turn, requires that the province assume control of the system.

3 *The scheme delivers an anti-urban bias in its impacts.*
A look at the Harris scheme abstracted from its political context begs two important questions. Why is the scheme so completely at variance with the recommendations of literally every review and study of the provincial/local government relationship in the province? And why, if the objective of the government was to reduce its financial commitment to education, did the province not either directly reduce its grants to school boards or (more subtly) force school boards to assume full responsibility for teacher pension costs?

The answer is that in these alternative approaches, the wrong areas of the province win — and the wrong areas of the province lose. Large urban areas in Ontario pay a disproportionate share of the municipal portion of social services costs. On the other hand, non-urban municipalities receive a disproportionate share of provincial grants for "hard" services. A reform along the lines recommended by the various reviews would tend to benefit larger urban municipalities and reduce the wide disparity in property tax burdens that currently benefits smaller municipalities.

In education, a simple reduction in grants would have no effect on Toronto and Ottawa and relatively little effect on larger urban boards like those in Sudbury, Hamilton and Windsor. Most of the impact would be felt in smaller, rural boards that are more heavily dependent on provincial grants.

Neither of these patterns of impact met the Harris Conservatives political objective of rewarding those parts of Ontario from which they drew most of their political support. Pushing social services spending down to municipalities and assuming control of education funding met the objective of concentrating the pain inflicted by the scheme in the right places politically – namely in Ontario's larger cities.

Information that has surfaced about the process by which the government arrived at its final package supports this view. Impact studies were apparently limited to broad regional data, often restricted to "Metro" and "everywhere else." Options were reportedly sent back over and over again because they didn't "get" Metro, Ottawa and other big cities enough. The anecdotes cannot be confirmed, but actions in this case speak louder than words. It is difficult to imagine a distribution of impacts of a reallocation of responsibilities that would be more unfriendly to areas of the province seen by this government to be politically unfriendly.

4. *The scheme shifts responsibility for services whose costs have been increasing and are likely to continue to increase in the future to municipalities and assumes provincial responsibility for education, where costs have been stable and are predictable.*

One of the few consistent patterns in the provincial offloading scheme is that the province has shifted areas of spending that have been growing rapidly over the past 10 years to municipalities. In contrast, the provincial government has assumed responsibility for a spending category – education – that has been growing very slowly.

Between 1986 and 1994, the most recent years for which

data are available, real per capita spending on social services increased at an annual rate of 16.5%, largely because of the early 1990s recession. Housing spending increased at an annual rate of 15%; child care at 15.1%. Real capita spending on education, by contrast, increased by only 1.3% – less than one-tenth as quickly.

By increasing municipal responsibilities for welfare (adding Family Benefits) and shifting all responsibility for housing and child care to municipalities, the Harris scheme transfers the spending areas that have been growing most quickly to the municipal level. These are also the spending categories most closely tied to general economic conditions – yet they have been transferred to the level of government with the narrowest and most regressive tax base. In return, the province assumes responsibility for education, the most stable, slowest growing and most recession-proof of the major spending areas at issue.

5. *The scheme sets up a political dynamic that the government expects will lead to further cuts in social services spending for which it will not have to take political responsibility.*

By increasing local governments' responsibility for these services, the scheme creates new opportunities for free riders. Many municipalities in Ontario already resort to various forms of "bus ticket welfare" to export their social services costs to major urban areas. There are already significant differences in local spending on social services from municipality to municipality in Ontario as a result. The relatively modest incentives to do so in the current system will be considerably enhanced in the new scheme.

That dynamic at the local government level will be reinforced at the individual taxpayer level. By shifting responsibility for funding social services down to local governments whose only fiscal resource is the property tax (the most regressive form of taxation), the Harris scheme is increasing the burden on ordinary working families of paying for these services. The government is evidently counting on taxpayer resistance to the tax increases that will inevitably result from its "reform" scheme to put further downward pressure on community standards in Ontario. The government is counting on a race to the bottom in community standards for public services, and Mike Harris has fired the starting gun.

What the Harris Scheme Does That They Haven't Told Us About

1. *Buried under seemingly modest shifts in regional average impacts, many municipalities and school boards will experience crippling increases in program and capital spending obligations, and devastating cuts in available resources.*

The local government sector in Ontario is extremely diverse. While it is generally true that large urban areas will bear the brunt of the impact of the trade of education for social services and housing responsibilities, Toronto and Ottawa aren't the only areas with high education and social services costs. And when the fact that the trade-off is by no means revenue neutral is factored in – the province is a net winner to the tune of nearly $1 billion – there will be significant losers throughout the province in municipalites of all sizes.

2. *Provincial control of education funding will result in massive cuts in education spending overall, concentrated in the hardest-to-serve areas.*

None of the studies of our education system has ever suggested that we are spending too much on elementary and secondary education in Ontario, nor have they suggested that the highest-cost areas are spending money unnecessarily. What they have suggested is that urgent action is necessary to address funding-related quality issues in revenue-poor boards. Such a reduction in financial commitment to education flies in the face of a consensus that Ontario's economic future depends critically in increasing rather than reducing our financial commitment to education.

3. *The move to market value assessment and the abolition of the business occupancy tax will create chaos in local government finance and increase property taxes for residents and small business owners.*

The business occupancy tax currently raises $1.6 billion on a sliding scale in which small businesses pay about a third less than the average tax and banks and other large businesses pay as much as 50% more. The extra tax paid by banks and big business will have to be paid by residential and small business taxpayers. Hundreds of millions of dollars in taxes will be shifted.

The shift to market value assessment itself will not be smooth. The government likes to cite data that purport to show that, outside Metro, the shifts in tax resulting from market value reassessment will be small. For individual taxpayers, that is simply not true. While it is true that the majority of municipalities in Ontario have been reassessed, those municipalities do not represent a majority of Ontario's population. And most of the municipalities that have been reassessed are working on reassessed tax bases that are as far out of date now as Toronto's was when the provincial government took over the assessment function from municipalities in the late 1960s. Millions of Ontario residents face substantial tax increases as a result of market value reassessment. The government knows it, but refuses to release the impact studies.

4. *The Harris scheme will damage fundamentally the foundation of the quality of life in Ontario for which this province has become so celebrated around the world.*

Ontario and its largest urban area have come out on top of international survey after international survey as the best place to live in the world. It is absolutely clear in looking closely at those surveys that the extent and quality of our public services plays a major role in establishing that reputation. The Harris scheme will increase economic inequality at the same time as it reduces our investment in our future and undermines the public services we depend on from day to day.

Strengthening Community Standards and Mutual Responsibility Through Partnerships

The basic premise of provincial/local disentanglement in its purest form is that there is something wrong with a system in which the provincial government and local governments share policy, financial and administrative responsibility for the same services. The theory suggests that better services could be delivered more efficiently and with greater accountability if they were reallocated between levels of government in accordance with a consistent set of principles.

We take issue with the basic premise that there is something wrong with shared responsibility for public services. There is nothing inherently wrong with a system of partnerships and shared responsibility for the design and delivery of public services.

The theory that the public interest is best served when only one level of government is responsible for any given service is unable to answer two important questions. If the logic of non-entanglement is so blindingly clear, why is it that – almost without exception – the development of public services in Ontario has involved partnerships among provincial governments, local governments and provincial and local non-profit organizations? Were the provincial and local leaders who created those partnerships stupid, or were they achieving something in public policy that could not have been achieved by either level of government acting alone?

And if the theory of disentanglement is so compelling in its logic, why is it that every review claiming to pursue that logic recommended *redefining* the interrelationships among governments in policy, finance and administration rather than *eliminating* those interrelationships?

The genius of the Ontario system of provincial/local government services as it has evolved over time is that by building on partnerships between levels of government, it has allowed public services to develop at different rates in different parts of Ontario, and has encouraged local innovation while ensuring that there continues to be steady progress in general provincial standards. Standards of public services would improve in some areas as local governments introduced innovative new programs. Provincial governments would often follow their lead, and provide financial support that enabled other local governments to move towards a higher standard of service.

Provincial objectives in areas like environmental quality and economic efficiency were served by the introduction of cost-sharing arrangements for sewer and water services and public transit. Programs like junior kindegarten and English as a Second Language were introduced in first a few school boards and then, as the merit of these programs was demonstrated, added to the range of programs supported by the provincial government.

The local dimension to these evolving partnerships makes local services more responsive to local needs. Local programs like AIDS awareness were a feature of the local public health systems in Ottawa and Toronto long before the issue was addressed in provincial programming. It also acts as a safety valve against the possibility that the central provincial bureaucracy may not get it right all the time. Without the substantial scope for local action built into the current system for funding education in Ontario, for example, it is unlikely that education in Toronto, Ottawa or Sudbury would have responded nearly as effectively to the needs of their increasingly diverse student populations.

The provincial dimension ensures that successful innovations are generalized, that everyone in Ontario benefits from a minimum standard of public services, and that local services are delivered in a way that is consistent with broader public policy objectives. It is difficult to see, for example, how Ontario could meet its commitments in such areas as water quality without an active provincial effort to improve sewer and water treatment standards. The vital partnerships that have built Ontario's system of public services are being sacrificed to pay for an ill-advised cut in personal income taxes. When even the Toronto Board of Trade tells the government that's a bad deal, something is clearly wrong.

That is not to say that the current arrangements are ideal. Ontario relies far too heavily on property taxes for education funding – much more heavily than other provinces. Ontario also relies too heavily on property taxes to fund social services. In this respect too, the Harris Government is moving in the opposite direction. When all the impacts are taken into account, education and social services together will be more heavily funded from property taxes than ever.

Partnerships cannot be written in stone. They evolve over time. The right balances have to be maintained between tax fairness and local initiative; between local control and flexibility and the need to ensure consistent high standards of public services.

From time to time these partnerships must be renovated and even rebuilt. But to destroy the provincial/local partnerships that built public services in this province and to reject even the idea of partnership, is to undermine the foundation of public programing in our society.

Chapter Thirteen

ONTARIO 1997-98 BUDGET HIGHLIGHTS

Minister Ernie Eves brought down the 1997–98 Ontario budget on May 6, 1997. Here is a brief summary of the highlights from an Alternative Budget perspective. It includes some of the flaws in the budget which are more fully analysed in the preceding chapters.

The Deficit: The Vanishing Fiscal Crisis

The provincial deficit for the fiscal year ending March 31, 1997, came in at $7.5 billion ($700 million less than the expected $8.2 billion). Tax revenues turned out to be almost $2 billion higher than Eves had projected. However, the government in the last months of the year added some $1.4 billion in additional restructuring costs to the 1996–97 budget (in essence, "paying in advance" severance and lay-off costs that will not be incurred until next year and after). This was done to prevent the deficit from looking too small. So the true deficit for 1996–97 was just $5.1 billion – or $2.1 billion below plan.

Since becoming finance minister, Ernie Eves has been deliberately making the deficit numbers look worse than they are. This allows him to "justify" his cutbacks. It also allows him to look good when he overachieves his own deliberately pessimistic targets. In reality, Ontario's deficit problem could have been solved without the spending cutbacks.

Minister Eves will use the same "funny accounting" for next year. Once again, he has deliberately underestimated personal income tax revenue by about $2 billion. He has used deliberately pessimistic expectations regarding economic growth and interest rates. And he has given himself a $650 million "reserve cushion." Put all these factors together, and the true deficit for 1997–98 will likely come in as much as $3 billion below the planned $6.6 billion.

The Cutbacks: Shrinking the Public Sector

Despite the better-than-expected fiscal situation, Eves is pressing ahead with planned cutbacks. Total program spending is projected to fall next year by almost $3 billion. Here are some of the hardest-hit targets:

Community and Social Services	$177 million
Education	$124 million
Teacher's pension plan	$429 million
Municipal Affairs and Housing	$437 million
Transportation	$425 million
Natural Resources	$57 million

By the end of the next fiscal year, total provincial program spending will have fallen to just 12 percent of Ontario GDP. That's down from 15 percent in 1995. In other words, the real size of public programs in Ontario's economy will have been cut by fully one-fifth since the Harris government came to power.

Opening the Wallet?

The budget contains some much-publicized – although tiny – social spending initiatives: $40 million for a low-income child care tax credit; $27 million over four years to combat violence against women; $30 million over five years for learning-disabled children; $650 million over two years to support capital spending by schools; and $25 million over five years for community safety. The total cost of *all* five of these new programs next year will be less than $400 million, or a puny 0.7 percent of total planned spending.

More importantly, it is not *new* money that is actually being spent. For instance, the child care tax credit would be funded with money reallocated away from provincial welfare spending thanks to the new federal child benefit. The "new" classroom construction spending offsets less than one-third of the cutbacks to other education program and capital spending (cuts which this year, excluding new construction funding, will total $1.1 billion). The bottom line, despite these initiatives, is that overall funding for public programs is continuing to decline. The Tories have not "loosened the purse strings."

Health Care Spending

The government makes special mention of its plan to "increase" health care spending. The basic health care operating budget is frozen at $17.85 billion. Health care capital spending is increased by $60 million (to $242 million – still far lower than under the NDP government). And the government has budgeted another $450 million in restructuring costs (for severance pay and other costs arising from hospital closures and lay-offs). Total health spending therefore comes to just $18.5 billion (the highest ever, in nominal dollar terms). Is the Harris government really expanding health care funding?

First, it is unfair to consider restructuring and lay-off costs as a form of "health care funding." These are not costs of providing health services, they are one-time costs to the government of *cancelling* health services. The real health budget is just over $18 billion.

And even this level of funding, despite the claims of Ernie Eves, does not "protect" health services of Ontarians. Adjusted for inflation and for Ontario's growing population, the level of real per capita health care spending in Ontario will have fallen by the end of next year by 6.5%, compared to 1995. It will have declined by close to 15% from 1992 levels.

No wonder that Ontarians feel the quality of their health care is deteriorating – despite Ernie Eves' promise to "freeze" total health care spending. The decline in health care is clearly linked to budgetary cutbacks.

Creeping Austerity

Despite the efforts of Harris supporters to "spin" this budget as being "kinder and gentler," in reality the provincial government's program spending will continue to fall quite substantially, and the quality of public services will continue to deteriorate.

Nevertheless, opponents of the cutbacks can take some pleasure in noting that there were no new major cutbacks announced in this budget – and indeed that the Harris government felt *obliged* to try to present itself as being committed to preserving and expanding public programs.

Financial analysts had expected the government to implement up to $3 billion in further spending cuts. Now it appears that this will not occur. Clearly the government is looking ahead two years to the next election. It is concerned about public resistance to its cutbacks, public concern about deteriorating health care and education, and its second-place showing in the public opinion polls. While this budget is still mean-spirited, it is clearly not as bad as it could have been – and for this, we must thank the activism and hard work of the province-wide resistance movement.

Total program and capital spending next year will be almost $2 billion higher than was originally forecast in the Harris campaign's Common Sense Revolution program. By the following year (fiscal 1998–99), total spending will probably be $4 billion higher than forecast in the Common Sense Revolution. Total spending cuts will probably be $3–4 billion smaller than the Common Sense Revolution (and many financial analysts) anticipated.

So while this government has imposed tremendous hardship on most citizens of Ontario, it has now backed away from *some* of the cuts it was *prepared* to make (and would probably still *prefer* to make). Resistance to the cutbacks *has* made a difference.

The Tax Cut and Spending Cuts

The budget confirms that the provincial government will proceed with the third and fourth installments of the reduction in provincial income taxes. From July 1 of this year until the end of the year, Ontario tax will be collected at the rate of 47% of basic federal tax. Starting January 1, 1998, the rate will be cut again to 45% of federal tax.

For the fiscal year as a whole (April 1, 1997 to March 31, 1998) that means the average Ontario tax rate will equal 47% of the federal rate. The cost during the current fiscal year of these additional two phases of the tax cut will be $625 million. The cost during the current fiscal year of the *cumulative* tax cuts imposed to date is some $3.4 billion. The cost of the fully phased-in *complete* tax cut package (according to which the rate will drop to 40.5% of the federal tax rate by 1999) will exceed $5 billion per year.

There is virtually a dollar-for-dollar relationship between the revenues lost due to the tax cut and the program spending cuts being made at the same time. Program and capital spending during the current fiscal year is budgeted at $3.2 billion less than in fiscal 1994–95 (the last full fiscal year prior to the election of the Harris government). The tax cut will cost a total of $3.4 billion in this fiscal year.

The government therefore could have avoided *all* spending cutbacks, and balanced its budget even *faster* than it is now doing simply by keeping the income tax rate at its 1994 level. (In fact, by avoiding the extra restructuring costs associated with its cutbacks, which will total almost $3 billion by the end of this year, a no-cutbacks, no-tax-cut strategy would be *billions* of dollars ahead of Harris on deficit reduction.)

It is now clearer than ever that the spending cuts in Ontario are the price of the tax cut. They are not driven by the need to reduce the deficit. *Harris wants smaller government, not a balanced budget.*

Because each billion dollars of tax cut has been matched by a billion dollars of spending cuts, the stimulative impact of the tax cut is negated. In fact, the job losses resulting from the spending cuts are significantly greater than the jobs that will be created as a result of the tax cut. First, high-income earners save much of their tax cut, rather than spending it, thus reducing the stimulative impact. Second, consumer spending has a higher *import component* than government services, meaning that much of the stimulus of a tax cut leaks out of the Ontario economy.

Where are the Jobs?

It is no wonder, then, that the Harris government is so far behind its own timetable on job creation. It promised to create 725,000 jobs during its first term in office. Therefore, it should have created almost 300,000 jobs by now.

In fact, barely 100,000 jobs have been created in the first two years of the Harris government – and the province's unemployment rate has actually *increased* (from 8.6% in June 1995 to 9% in April 1997). The government is ahead of its schedule on deficit reduction, but 200,000 jobs behind its schedule for job-creation. This gives a good picture of this government's priorities.

It looks like 1997 will be a good year for job-creation in Canada – for reasons that have nothing to do with the Harris government. Low interest rates are finally having an impact, and exports to the U.S. continue to grow. But how long will this last? Interest rates are already rising, and the U.S. economy is slowing down. Thanks to high interest rates and government cutbacks, Canada's economic recovery since 1991 has been the weakest in the entire postwar era. If growth now stops in the U.S., our economy will slow down again: our recovery will be snuffed out before it really gets going.

We need sustained low interest rates, strong job creation, and growing personal incomes. The huge Harris cutbacks have exactly the opposite effect on our economy. And the tax cut does not come close to offsetting the continuing stagnation of wages in our private-sector economy.

Chapter Fourteen

THE ALTERNATIVE FEDERAL BUDGET AND ITS IMPLICATIONS FOR ONTARIO

History and Process

The Ontario Alternative Budget project owes much of its organizational and intellectual inspiration to a similar project that has been underway at the federal level for over three years. The first Alternative Federal Budget (AFB) was released in February 1995 to coincide with Finance Minister Paul Martin's historic cutbacks budget of that year. Since then, subsequent versions of the AFB have been released every spring. The 1997 AFB, together with a dense collection of background documents and technical papers, was published for the first time as a single volume: *The 1997 Alternative Federal Budget Papers* (Ottawa: Canadian Centre for Policy Alternatives).

The AFB is assembled by a coalition of over 50 national organizations representing organized labour, social policy and social justice advocates, and community organizations. The budget also benefits from the participation and input of numerous individual academics and policy researchers. Major decisions regarding the content and format of the AFB are made by a steering committee composed of representatives of the sponsoring organizations. More detailed policy development work is carried on by a number of specialized policy committees – addressing issues such as the AFB's macroeconomic and fiscal framework, job-creation, social policy, housing, and the environment. The overall project is co-sponsored by two organizations: the Canadian Centre for Policy Alternatives in Ottawa (a non-profit progressive research institute), and the CHO!CES social justice coalition based in Winnipeg (which initiated the alternative budget movement some years ago, by developing annual alternative budgets for the city of Winnipeg and the province of Manitoba).

Each successive version of the AFB has gained in public exposure (both through the mainstream media and through the education and outreach activities of supporting grass-roots organizations) and credibility. In addition, because the project is repeated each year, the level of detail and thoroughness of its policy analysis can be improved from year to year. Some topic areas are essentially repeated from one year to the next, while others receive further elaboration or revision. And whole new policy areas need to be addressed as new topics of public interest and controversy arise. For example, the upcoming 1998 version of the AFB will have several new policy and budgetary issues to address: What does the coming era of balanced budgets imply for the AFB and its supporters? How do we respond to business pressure for tax cuts? Will it be possible, now that the wave of anti-deficit hysteria is subsiding, to rebuild the scope of government and public services in Canada?

The AFB's Fiscal and Economic Framework

The central starting point of the AFB has been that social programs were not the cause of Canada's debt and deficit difficulties, and hence that slashing the funding base of these programs is neither a necessary nor a desirable means of solving those fiscal difficulties. The emergence of large chronic deficits for the federal government, and the resulting escalation of the federal debt burden, are instead rooted in the high real interest rates, high unemployment, and prolonged economic stagnation which Canada has experienced since the early 1980s.

By abandoning its commitment to full-employment, and putting top priority instead on reducing inflation and enhancing the real rates of return on financial assets, federal policy-makers themselves lit the fuse for the coming fiscal explosion of the mid-1990s. The sustained, deliberate macroeconomic slowdown of the past fifteen years put immediate pressure on the federal government's fiscal position: high unemployment and slow growth meant less government revenues, combined with higher expenses for unemployment insurance and other income support and social programs. And since the entire process was set in motion by dramatic increases in real interest rates, the federal budget was doubly damaged: the government's own interest charges (required to service a growing debt that was itself the primary result of high-interest-rate, anti-inflation policies), escalated dangerously.

To emphasize the point that it was high interest rates and unemployment – not social programs – that created the federal government's debt problem, the AFB has adopted a strategic if controversial fiscal stance. The AFB has accepted the *same timelines* for deficit reduction that were first spelled out by Paul Martin in the run-up to his 1995 budget, and which have been subsequently extended year-by-year.[1] But the AFB then showed how those same deficit targets could be met through a macroeconomic strategy emphasizing sustained growth, lower interest rates, and job creation – rather than the social pain and dislocation that have been the results of Paul Martin's budget-cutting crusade. In reality, because Paul Martin's targets were deliberately conservative (both the government and business analysts knew that the spending measures announced by Martin were far more than what was actually required to meet his stated targets), the AFB is actually about one year behind the Liberal government in reducing the deficit (since Martin is at least a year ahead of his own targets). But if Martin's targets themselves have any credibility whatsoever, then the AFB has shown that it is at least as "fiscally responsible" as the Liberal government, matching Martin's deficit targets point for point. In fact, in terms of the reduction of the federal *debt* burden as a share of GDP (which most economists now see as a more important goal than merely reducing the annual deficit), the AFB achieves *faster* debt-reduction than Paul Martin – thanks to the fiscal benefits of faster economic growth and job-creation.

The growth and job-creation strategy of the AFB is based on several key policy planks, including:

- reducing and maintaining the real interest rate on long-run government bonds to 3–4%, and on shorter-run instruments to 1–2%
- utilizing the Bank of Canada (the federal government's own bank) to play a more interventionist role in maintaining low interest rates and financing a larger share of federal government debt
- reversing the spending cuts and job losses in federal programs, and consequently reversing the spin-off job destruction that has occurred in the private sector
- the creation of an Emergency Employment Investment Program, with a budget of $6 billion over the first two years, to support up-front job-creation in rebuilding Canada's concrete, social, and environmental infrastructure
- establishing a public investment bank, whose initial seed capital is obtained from the compulsory deposit of a small share (eventually reaching 0.3%) of the assets of private financial institutions, to finance job-creating industrial and community development projects at the local, regional, and sectoral levels
- beginning to regulate flows of capital in other ways (for example, by eliminating the 20% of tax-subsidized RRSPs and pension funds that can currently be invested offshore), in support of the effort to maintain low interest rates and investment in Canada
- pursuing other methods (such as reduced work time

regulations in the federal jurisdiction) to enhance job-creation

As a result of these and other expansionary measures, the AFB anticipates that the real rate of growth of Canada's GDP can be increased by about 1 percentage point over the next five years (from the 2.5% rate envisioned as "sustainable" by most private forecasters, to an estimated 3.5% per year). The inflation rate is expected to increase by about 1 full percentage point as a result of faster growth and lower interest rates (from 2% in current consensus forecasts to 3% in the AFB scenario). Higher inflation and a lower Canadian dollar (expected to settle in the range of 70 U.S. cents) are the side-effects of the AFB's emphasis on sustained job-creation; but in fact, both of these "consequences" actually assist the effort to reduce the deficit (since higher inflation means higher government revenues) and create jobs (a lower dollar enhances the competitiveness of Canadian exports).

Budget Highlights

Thanks to faster growth and lower interest rates, the AFB is able to meet Paul Martin's own timetable for deficit reduction, while still reversing the painful cutbacks in federal program spending that Martin has overseen. The key fiscal highlights of the 1997 AFB are summarized below in Table 14.1 (which also provides a comparison with the actual federal budget for 1997-98).

The AFB increases total program spending by $16 billion above the Martin budget for the fiscal year 1997-98, and by $24 billion above Martin for the following year. While these seem like large increases, in reality they only represent the reversal of the spending cutbacks that Martin has implemented since 1995. Total AFB program spending of $121.7 billion in the current fiscal year only equals the $118 billion that the federal government was spending prior to the cutbacks (in fiscal 1994-95), plus an additional $3 billion in the Emergency Employment Investment Program.

Unlike the Liberals, the sponsors of the AFB recognize that

reducing the deficit is not the only budgetary task of the federal government. Therefore, in addition to its targets for deficit and debt reduction, the AFB also sets itself targets for two important *social* indicators: the unemployment rate and the poverty rate. The AFB argues that the federal government should attach the same attention and determination to meeting these targets – "come hell or high water" – as it does to reducing the final deficit. Thanks to rapid job creation and to the rebuilding of income support programs and other anti-poverty programs, the AFB intends to reduce Canada's unemployment rate to 7% by the end of fiscal 1998 (and lower in subsequent years), and the poverty rate to no more than 14.5% (compared to the present 19%) in the same time frame.

The AFB contains several innovative proposals in the area of social policy. Federal support for health, education, welfare, pensions, and other public services (some of which currently fall within provincial jurisdiction) is rebuilt through the establishment of seven different National Social Investment Funds. Each fund is based on a distinct funding formula (including, where appropriate, cost-sharing with provincial governments), and each contains measures allowing for the enforcement of high national standards in the delivery of each respective public service.

Implications for Ontario

The adoption of expansionary, full-employment macroeconomic and budgetary policies at the federal level would make immeasurably easier the task of resolving Ontario's current fiscal difficulties in a humane and progressive fashion. The benefits of an AFB-style federal strategy would "trickle down" to Ontario's budgeters in several different ways:[2]

- Direct increases in federal transfer payments to support provincially-managed public services (such as health care and post-secondary education). Under the AFB, Ontario would receive an *additional* $2.1 billion in the current fiscal year (compared to actual federal transfers), and more in subsequent years.

- Faster job-creation. The AFB would increase total employment by an additional 150,000-200,000 jobs per year. Some 60,000-80,000 of these new jobs created *each year* would be located in Ontario, helping to bring the provincial unemployment rate down to 6% or lower by the end of the fiscal year 1998-99 (even *before* considering the job-creation benefits of an Ontario Alternative Budget). Lower unemployment in Ontario means higher tax revenues and lower social welfare expenses for the provincial government.
- Thanks both to faster job-creation and to progressive adjustments to the federal income tax structure (including new tax brackets for high-income earners, and a new wealth transfer tax for millionaires), the AFB would result in an automatic increase in *provincial* income tax revenues of at least $1 billion per year.
- The creation and maintenance of lower interest rates in Canada would also reduce Ontario's annual interest charges. The 2 point reduction in real interest rates envisioned by the AFB could eventually save the provincial government up to $1 billion per year on its own interest payments.

In sum, Ontario's provincial balance would be improved by some $4 billion per year (and more in future years) by the implementation of an AFB strategy at the federal level. When one considers that the total provincial deficit in 1996-97 (excluding one-time restructuring charges resulting from the spending cuts themselves) was just over $5 billion, then it becomes clear that the *provincial* fiscal problem would – in essence – be almost completely cured by a reversal of neo-conservative direction at the *federal* level. Indeed, this conclusion is quite consistent with our emphasis that it was not provincial "overspending," but rather an incredibly hostile macroeconomic environment (high interest rates, an overvalued dollar, free trade, and cuts in federal transfers), that created Ontario's huge deficits of the early 1990s. It follows, then, that a reversal of those restrictive federal policies would similarly resolve the difficulties these policies caused at lower levels of government.[3]

Of course, given the continued neo-conservative policy direction being followed by the federal Liberal government, it is unlikely that few, if any, AFB-style budgetary measures will be implemented by this government in the foreseeable future. For this reason (as discussed above in Chapter 2), the Ontario Alternative Budget project cannot count on the fiscal benefits of a restoration of pro-growth, full-employment policies at the federal level. This makes the task of rebuilding Ontario's finances, while preserving and ultimately expanding our base of public programs and services, all the harder. Nevertheless, the political struggle to reverse the harsh policies of fiscal restraint needs to be carried to all levels of government in Canada – and hence the symmetries between the Ontario Alternative Budget and its older, federal "sibling" are worth emphasizing.

Table 14.1 A Tale of Two Budgets: Paul Martin vs. The Alternative Budget

	Fiscal 1997–98 Martin	Fiscal 1997–98 Alternative	Fiscal 1998–99 Martin	Fiscal 1998–99 Alternative
Budget Highlights				
Program Spending	$105.8 b	$121.7 b	$103.5 b	$128.7 b
Change Previous Yr.	–$3.2 b	+$13.6 b	–$2.3 b	+$7.0 b
Tax Revenues	$137.8 b	$147.8 b	$144.0 b	$160.2 b
Change Previous Yr.	+$2.3 b	+$13.5 b	+$6.2 b	+$12.4 b
Debt Service Charges	$46.0 b	$42.8 b	$46.5 b	$41.1 b
Deficit	$17.0 b[†]	$16.6 b	$9.0 b[†]	$9.6 b
Deficit/GDP	2.0%[†]	1.9%	1.0%[†]	1.0%
Debt/GDP	71.8%	71.3%	69.9%	67.7%
Macroeconomic Conditions				
Real GDP Growth	3.2%	4.0%	2.6%	4.1%
Inflation	1.6%	2.4%	1.8%	2.8%
90-day Interest Rate	4.0%	3.1%	4.5%	3.5%

	Fiscal 1997–98		Fiscal 1998–99	
	Martin	Alternative	Martin	Alternative
Employment and Poverty Targets				
Jobs Created	300,000?	460,000	300,000?	500,000
Unemployment Target	None	8.6%	None	7.0%
Poverty Target	None	16.5%	None	14.5%

† These are the official budget estimates (including contingency reserve funds and conservative macroeconomic assumptions). The actual federal deficit is likely to be $10–$12 billion (or slightly over 1% of GDP) in 1997–98, and zero in 1998–99.

Endnote

1 Martin pledged successively to reduce the federal deficit to no more than 3% of GDP by the fiscal year 1996, 2% by 1997, and 1% by 1998. In reality, all of these targets have been considerably over-achieved.

2 These are discussed further in Chapter 2, "Options for Restoring Ontario's Fiscal Capacity," and in particular the description there of Scenario Four.

3 As illustrated in Scenario Four in Chapter 2, an AFB-style federal policy would allow the maintenance of pre-Harris public spending in Ontario (in constant real per capita terms), with no provincial tax increases and a balanced budget by the year 2000.

The Our Schools/Our Selves Series

James Lorimer & Company is now distributing and marketing the Our Schools/Our Selves book series. New titles will be published as series titles. The backlist of titles is now available to the trade through James Lorimer & Company. *Our Schools/Our Selves* subscribers will continue to receive copies of these titles as they are published, as part of their *OS/OS* subscription. Libraries and bookstores can order *Our Schools/Our Selves* from James Lorimer & Company through its distributor:

Formac Distributing Limited
5502 Atlantic Street
Halifax B3H 1G4
Toll free order line 1-800-565-1975
Fax orders (902) 425-0166

In the U.S.:
Formac Distributing Limited
121 Mount Vernon Street
Boston MA 02108
1-800-565-1975

Contact the order desk to be sure to receive your copy of the 1997 Lorimer university catalogue

Subscribe & Save

Please enter my subscription for 6 issues of OUR SCHOOLS/OUR SELVES starting with issue number _____. Please check one:

INDIVIDUAL
____ Regular rate $38.00
____ Student/Unemployed/
       Pensioner rate $32.00
____ Outside Canada   Cdn $50.00

ORGANIZATION
____ In Canada $50.00
____ Outside Canada   Cdn $60.00

SUSTAINING
____ $100   ____ $200   Other $____

OR send me issue number(s) _____ at $9.00 per single and $16.00 per double issue

To subscribe please phone our toll-free number at 1-800-565-1975 or mail form to *Our Schools/Our Selves*, 5502 Atlantic Street, Halifax, NS B3H 9Z9

Name _____
Address _____
City _____ Prov _____ Code _____
Occupation _____
          ❏ Cheque enclosed   ❏ VISA/Mastercard
Card No. _____ Expiry Date _____
Signature _____

Pass to a Friend

Please enter my subscription for 6 issues of OUR SCHOOLS/OUR SELVES starting with issue number _____. Please check one:

INDIVIDUAL
____ Regular rate $38.00
____ Student/Unemployed/
       Pensioner rate $32.00
____ Outside Canada   Cdn $50.00

ORGANIZATION
____ In Canada $50.00
____ Outside Canada   Cdn $60.00

SUSTAINING
____ $100   ____ $200   Other $____

OR send me issue number(s) _____ at $9.00 per single and $16.00 per double issue

To subscribe please phone our toll-free number at 1-800-565-1975 or mail form to *Our Schools/Our Selves*, 5502 Atlantic Street, Halifax, NS B3H 9Z9

Name _____
Address _____
City _____ Prov _____ Code _____
Occupation _____
          ❏ Cheque enclosed   ❏ VISA/Mastercard
Card No. _____ Expiry Date _____
Signature _____